A SOUTHERN MODERATE SPEAKS

A
SOUTHERN
MODERATE SPEAKS

BY

BROOKS HAYS

CHAPEL HILL

The University of North Carolina Press

Hays, Brooks. A southern moderate speaks. Chapel Hill, University of
North Carolina Press [1959]   231 p.   21 cm.   1. U. S.—Race question.
2. Negroes—Civil rights.   3. Negroes—Little Rock, Ark.   4. Segregation
in education.   I. Title.   E185.61.H435   301.451   59–9064 ‡   Library of
Congress

MANUFACTURED IN THE UNITED STATES OF AMERICA
VAN REES PRESS • NEW YORK

Dedicated to

My wife Marion

Our daughter Betty

and

Our son Steele

*Who have given me unfailing encouragement and sympathy
in the exertions that produced this book*

"Let your moderation be known unto all men."

PHIL. 4:5

Foreword

My INTEREST IN RACE RELATIONS BEGAN IN MY BOYHOOD AND
has continued through several turbulent political campaigns
to the present moment. When the issues were thrust into the
Congress and the national party conventions, an urge to help
find solutions propelled me into the center of the conflict, and
I have tried to find the proper balance between moral and
political considerations. This effort is described in some of
the pages that follow.

I believe that the title of this book is an honest one. Labels
are often deceptive but the word "moderation" as generally
used fits my approach. And I am a Southerner. I speak as an
American, too, and as one who believes that sectional conflicts can be harmonized and that the national interest can
be conserved through an appeal to reason and to reasonableness on both sides.

One reason for my actions in the Little Rock crisis and the
continuing controversy over civil rights is that, having sensed
the strength of the political forces generated outside the
South, I have wanted to spare the people of my city and
region the pain and discomfort that would follow any mis-
judgments of political attitudes and public sentiment in other
parts of the United States.

This is the story exactly as written before the eight-day write-in campaign that cost me my seat in Congress in November, 1958. The significant events connected with that campaign, in which my opponent had the support of Governor Faubus, belong to another narrative. Relief from Congressional duties gives me an opportunity to devote more time to educational and religious endeavors and will, I hope, also enable me to write a sequel bringing this narrative to a satisfying and successful conclusion. The hope for such a conclusion is brighter as the result of the recent Supreme Court decision upholding Alabama's pupil placement act. This shows that the justices are scrutinizing the complexities of the segregation issue more closely and are anxious to make their adherence to principle as flexible in practice as is compatible with the need for national unity.

One thing that I hope this story will accomplish is the dispelling of any impression that some might entertain that I was consulted regarding the sending of troops to Little Rock, or that I shared in that decision.

Another reason for telling the complete story is that portions of it as reported in segmented form from my speeches have sometimes produced a distorted picture. On occasion I have even been judged harshly by fellow Southerners for suggesting possible alteration of Southern patterns and have not been credited with accompanying efforts to change sentiment outside the South. Pride in my position as a Southern moderate has therefore influenced me to write this book. I recognize, of course, that moderation is not always a virtue. Truth is often partisan, and reality in its unpleasant aspects must be confronted if we are to make progress. But one may express strong conviction without doing damage to the ideal of moderation. The word itself is mentioned but once in the Bible, and very favorably, by Paul, who said to the Philippians, "Let your moderation be known unto all men." He also said to the Ephesians, "Speak the truth in love," and both injunctions seem to fit our times.

Words fail me in attempting to express my profound appreciation to Warren I. Cikins, my legislative assistant, who has devoted much time and effort to helping me express my views and to assembling the data for this manuscript. His great abilities have been an invaluable asset to me. I am also grateful to the other members of my staff, John S. McLees, Mrs. Lurlene Wilbert, and Miss Kitty Johnson, for their splendid assistance. And finally I should like to pay tribute to the outstanding editorial help provided by the staff of The University of North Carolina Press.

B. H.
December 1, 1958

Contents

A SOUTHERN MODERATE SPEAKS

CHAPTER ONE

The Roar Beyond Silence

"IF WE HAD A KEEN VISION AND FEELING OF ALL ORDINARY human life, it would be like hearing the grass grow and the squirrel's heartbeat, and we should die of that roar which lies on the other side of silence." I began this book many years ago, but the impetus to finish it came to me only re- cently during a walk from the Congressional office building to the Capitol. It was one of those delightful autumn days that Washingtonians enjoy, and a friend with whom I like to discuss the philosophy of government was walking with me. We almost stumbled across a squirrel burying a nut in the middle of a wide grassy area. When I raised the question as to how he would ever find that morsel of food, a Capitol policeman, who was enjoying the sight himself, assured us that he would find it all right. He had seen squirrels retrieve their food under all kinds of circumstances. He even recalled seeing one dig through a light layer of snow for a buried nut. My friend supplemented the policeman's knowledge of the life and habits of squirrels.

Suddenly I remembered the words of George Eliot about the "roar," and I found this concept had a new meaning in the context of the struggle of all forms of life for survival and worth and dignity. Only the title of this chapter is new, for

1

the conclusions recorded here grew out of a lifetime's observations and reflections. One would think from looking at the publishers' lists that a lot of politicians write books, but nothing like as many write them as talk and dream of doing it. I remember, for example, going with a friend, with whom I served on a committee to draft a farm homestead law for Arkansas, to discuss our problem with the late Governor Carl Bailey, who had given us the assignment. While we were waiting to see the Governor my friend said, "I am going to write a book about this project." I told him then about the manuscript I had in mind, dealing with race relations. Imagine how we felt when the Governor began the conference by saying, "I think I'll get busy on a book that needs to be written." Each of us fought for the floor a few minutes to tell about his book, and that part of the conference ended with the unanimous agreement that the quotation on a stone reputed to have been unearthed by archeologists in ancient Babylon just about spoke the truth: "Conditions are gradually getting worse; children no longer obey their parents, and every man wants to write a book."

The Governor wanted to begin his book with a statement on the limitations which confront men in public office. "I thought when I became Governor," he said, "that all I needed to do would be to *will* to do good, that sitting at this desk I could order things done, and that the power centered here would be so great that the will to do them would achieve the result."

How different the exercise of governmental power really is. The chief difficulty is that the minds of people are so seldom fully conditioned to accept the means required to achieve the goals which so many would really like to reach. Sir Henry Maine summed it up: "Social opinion must be in advance of law; and the greater or less happiness of the people depends on the narrowness of the gap."

The great jurist was making two points. First he was saying that unless the people themselves have yielded their sentiments and their will to a proposed law, the putting of a measure on the statute books does not bring achievement. But he added something that should be a challenge to those who make and execute our laws, that the great job of the political profession is to narrow the gap between law and custom, whichever may, at the particular moment in history, be in advance of the other. It has seemed to me that my own story, particularly my work in race relations, is a story of a lifetime of adventures in that gap between law and custom. As an illustration, let me show how one of the major transformations that has already taken place in the South has affected my own political career.

In 1928, the year of my first candidacy for the governorship of Arkansas, I reached three hundred communities for formal speaking engagements. On the fringe of one of those small audiences I saw a number of Negro listeners silently pondering the things I said about improving the lot of farm people, wondering, I assume, if they would be included in the benefits that the ambitious young would-be governor proposed. Their faces haunted me. I knew, of course, that even if they were favorably impressed, they would not be given a voice in the electoral processes. They would have no opportunity to record these impressions. Their silent resentments were not heard, but the roar was forming and it would be heard—earlier than many of us thought. And the winning of the franchise for the Southern Negro, now widely conceded, was not only the first of the notable forward steps in his new emancipation; it would prove to be the key to his progress in many fields.

Negro participation in Southern elections is generally credited to the Supreme Court decision outlawing the white primary. It should have been apparent, though, that even before that decision many party leaders in the South were recognizing the problem and arguing for a liberalization of party rules. This evolutionary process was being stimulated by the growth of Republican strength in the region. The necessity for concessions to the Negro to prevent mass support of Republican candidates in the fall elections was resulting in a change of Democratic policy on Negro voting in the primaries when the Supreme Court decision settled the matter.

It is not accurate, of course, to assert that it is a settled question, since in many areas custom has not caught up with the Court, but it has become a judicial problem rather than a political one, with federal policy secondarily involved. These policy questions exacerbate the whole civil rights legislative controversy. I can fully sympathize with the Negro's impatience with delays in permitting him to vote in primaries of "the party of his choice" which led him to resort to court action. Still, I deplore the fact that this gain was at the cost of impairing the principle that political parties should be granted maximum freedom in determining their procedures and policies even in so vital a matter as racial distinctions in membership. This may be regarded as theoretical, even legalistic, but I cannot avoid this feeling that the decision's having been made by the Court in Washington rather than by scattered party committees robs us of something that a free political society might well treasure in the present test of our system. The end results are good, however, for I am convinced that John Locke was right: "There can be no government *of* and *for* the people unless there is government *by* the people."

Many white Southerners agree that Negro voting "had to come" even without the Court action. It might be said to be a matter of conscience with sensitive people who were shocked by the affront to the individual Negro in the denial of the vote—even in Mississippi where white Southerners have insisted that widespread and sudden admission to the ballot would pose new and severe problems for many communities. Time becomes a mediator, but the matter will be finally resolved on the principle of permitting no one, whatever his race or social status, to be denied so basic a right as the vote. Again, it is the element of human dignity that should give greatest weight.

Theorizing aside, it is obvious that the Negro's access to democratic primaries is a profound new influence. My own experience is a fair demonstration of the fact. In 1942 when I made my second race for Congress (nine years after a heartbreaking first attempt on the heels of two defeats for the governorship), the single issue raised by my opponent, the lieutenant governor of the state, was that I would seek to alter the Negro's status. It was regarded as a vote-getting charge and obviously there were no counter advantages for me since the Negroes were not able to vote. Ten years later my 1952 opponent, entertaining the same race views as my 1942 opponent, uttered not a word with reference to my interest in the race problem. The reason: more than twelve thousand Negroes were paying the poll tax in the district and a majority of them were voting in the primary.

In subsequent chapters I shall have something to say about the possibility of emancipating local civic and educational leadership from the restraints that have resulted in some localities from irrational reactions to the Supreme Court decisions in the educational cases. It is my prediction that Russellville, Arkansas, my home town, will be among those communities which find a way to comply with the decision even in the absence of clarifying rulings which, from the standpoint of the over-all solution, are needed. The school officials of Russellville, including elected board members, would doubtless like to do away with a procedure which requires Negro high-school students to make a fifty-mile roundtrip bus ride each day to attend an all-Negro high school.

I heard one outspoken opponent of federally forced integration concede, "A student has a right to go to school in his own community—regardless of how much it inconveniences a community to give him school opportunities." And he added in what was almost a concurrence with the Court, "Anyway, how can a community oppose admitting such a small percentage of Negro students?"

Russellville, where I was born just before the turn of the century, is the county seat of Pope County, in the Ozark foothills. At that time the town had a population of three thousand, of whom one fourth were Negroes. I cannot offer the experience of a western Arkansas town as typical of that vast area we call the Old South. However, a boyhood spent in a small community in which one person in four lived in "colored town" produced opinions and sympathies—and perhaps some prejudices that can fairly be described as Southern.

My first recollections of Little Rock, which was later to be my home, go back to January, 1901, when I was two years old and heard the "clap clap" of horses' feet on the brick pavement of Center Street, which led from the old State House through a Negro residential section to what is now the Governor's Mansion. My father was chief clerk of the House of Representatives—"the state legislature" it was always called—and my parents and I, the only child, stopped at the Gleason Hotel, the Gadsby Tavern of Arkansas politics. From that day in 1901 Little Rock noises have never ceased to fascinate me, but Little Rock has its meaningful silences, too. Actually I have never heard anyone speak of Little Rock as a noisy city. And my childish mind sensed no incipient roars of discontent on the race front.

It was a period of unexpressed hopes—faint hopes by Negroes for a better scheme. But resentments were patiently borne, and good will between the races was more than surface deep. The first decade of the twentieth century has recently been described by a distinguished Negro historian as constituting the nadir in the fortunes of his race following the Civil War. In the South, by the early nineteen hundreds, the disfranchising of the Negroes who had been given the vote in Reconstruction had been completed. The Jim Crow laws in public accommodations and transportation, enacted during the latter decades of the preceding century, had achieved the sanction of approval by the Supreme Court. Public education in the South was in its infancy even for the whites, and for the Negroes it was almost non-existent. In the North the Republican party, which had come into existence to right the wrongs of slavery, had in the fleshpots of material prosperity let the Negro become its forgotten man.

That is undoubtedly good history, by and large, but I did not know it in 1910. Probably few white people in Russellville at that time were aware of any interest in politics on the part of its Negro citizens, but my boundless curiosity regarding the life of my Negro friends who lived to themselves in the lower end of town developed the fact that at least one of them, our elderly part-time yard man, not only had observing and sensitive eyes and ears for the politics of the period but a comprehensive if crude and unprecise knowledge of the politics of the slavery and Reconstruction periods.

One day I inquired of him: "Uncle Nelson, why are you a Republican?" (The use of the term Uncle and Aunt in addressing Negro elders is not in favor with the Negro people today and their wishes are generally respected. While their feelings today are understandable, I am confident that in the period in which the practice grew up it was recognized by all as a device for showing respect and affection.) The fine old man, who doubtless had never discussed politics with a white person before, stroked his carefully trimmed white beard, and I think he was pleased even though the question was addressed to him by a twelve-year-old boy. His answer was ready. "You see," he said, "the Republican party is the party of freedom—the Democratic party is the party of bondage." He did not elaborate upon that short emphatic answer and I did not pursue the matter, but it made a lasting impression. Even then, my Democratic loyalties were well developed, but my respect for the old man was so great that I resolved to learn more about the facts on which he based his surprisingly candid answer.

I was equally curious about Jim Crow. A train trip stimulated my thinking on the subject. Indelibly fixed in my memory is a trip with my father to Little Rock, a journey of seventy-five miles and rare enough to be an event. An overflow of Negro passengers necessitated bringing some of them into one of the coaches reserved for white passengers, and the conductor, to comply with state law and custom, placed a rope across the aisle. Before we reached Little Rock the Negroes had filled all of their seats and were crowding the portion of the aisle reserved for them. There were many vacant seats in our section but no one removed the rope or placed it further toward the rear. It would have been unthinkable not to have some symbol of compliance with the law which no white man of that period, and perhaps few Negroes, had heard openly criticized. I recall, however, that one Negro man seemed to register contempt for the treatment. Pressed against the rope, he could have touched empty seats reserved for whites and he could see a score of others behind them. We rode in physical comfort but I was not mentally at ease. Even now that Negro passenger's look haunts me. I could not speak to my father about it, for though he was, by the period's standards, liberal, he might have regarded me as nurturing strange ideas about Southern customs. There were roars on that Russellville-Little Rock train that day that were not attributable to the locomotive or the grinding wheels. But we were not to hear them for decades.

In 1915 I entered the University of Arkansas at Fayetteville, then a town of 7,500 people. Race problems did not engage me to an appreciable extent, though on occasions I gazed down from East Mountain into Tincup where the town's few Negroes lived and I was curious. At that time it was regarded as an innocent star-gazing practice among university people to talk of a better break for the Negro population. It was a reflection of the spirit of the times, and no one was thought to be subversive who began to raise questions about full justice for the Negro. The YMCA asked me to conduct a voluntary informal class on race relations at our fraternity house and the brothers agreed to cooperate. I think they did it partly to humor me but the point is that it was not shocking to the fraternity men, most of whom came from economically favored families.

Upon graduation from the University of Arkansas I decided to attend the evening classes of George Washington University Law School and, through the intervention of my congressman, H. M. Jacoway, secured a job in the Treasury Department at $1200 a year. I arrived in Washington in the late afternoon of Sunday, July 19, 1919, and went to the old Metropolitan Hotel. I sensed a feeling of tension as I walked along Pennsylvania Avenue and attributed it to my own mood of bewilderment, but when a troop of cavalrymen rode solemnly along the avenue I made some inquiries and learned that I had reached the capital at the peak of a race riot. Then the price of the $3.00 room did not seem exorbitant and I stayed inside while some belated skirmishing took place.

During a substantial number of the intervening years I have had a home in Washington and I have never known such violence as that of 1919. The Washington situation was fairly typical of conflicts in the northern and border cities of the period following World War I and represents a sharp contrast with the condition following the second World War. We have made progress in race relations.

In my first three years in Washington I was busy with the Treasury clerkship and my law studies and took little notice of changing conditions in the capital city. (One of my banker friends described that job like this: "Brooks counts $20 bills all day long, eight hours a day, six days a week, and on Saturday night he gets one of them.") I do remember turning down membership in the Ku Klux Klan which had excited considerable interest among the college students. The enrollment of a nephew of Imperial Wizard Simmons in our law class sharpened interest, but my Arkansas schoolmates took the same view I did—the Klan was nineteenth century. We were determined to live in the twentieth.

In June of 1922 I took my Arkansas bride of four months back to Russellville to practice law, and for two and a half years was the decidedly junior member of my father's three-man firm. If I was not the big man at the law office I was at least, through expenditure of considerable energy, quite a figure in the Baptist Church. Our pastor was a Klansman and I found it necessary to oppose not only him but a lot of boyhood friends in that misguided movement that brought to some in the South terror and physical injury, to others only bitterness and a hurt to the spirit.

The Klan elected a lot of county officers in Arkansas between 1920 and 1928, and even an occasional congressman and a state officer. I attribute my father's defeat for Congress in 1922 partly to his refusal to join the Russellville Klan.

Still our community was spared the more severe forms of racial antagonism and upon the dissolution of the local Klan, even before the national organization collapsed, I tended to lose interest in the race problem. I believe that one of the most unfortunate results of the Klan activity was to freeze the existing relationships by discouraging Negro cohesiveness for self advancement and any demonstration by the white majority of sympathy with their group aspirations. During our residence in Russellville I was active not only in the little church but in the Lions and other civic clubs, and I recall now with a feeling of deep regret that I did little to help make the white leadership conscious of a social problem at our doorstep. This general apathy was not altogether due to lack of imagination by the "ruling" class—it was also rooted in the deficiencies of the Negro leadership of the period. If they could have found a way to marshal their limited resources for urging improvement of opportunities for their young people, for example, I am confident there would have been a sympathetic response on the part of those who might have helped them.

My contacts with members of the Negro community rarely ever involved an observation of their collective life. In Arkansas at that time white people usually did not attend Negro gatherings—both races were a bit self-conscious when it occurred. (Fortunately for good race relations, this is changing.) One exception was the occasional talk at church service by a white minister or layman, and my lawyer father filled the role admirably. I went with him for that purpose one Sunday evening to the New Bethlehem Baptist Church. When my father finished his talk, there was the usual response from the congregation. Deacon Hendrix was asked to "respond" and he did it without rhetorical inhibitions. He could not have made his point otherwise. "I'm so glad Brother Hays came to us. He has stirred our hearts, he has exalted our souls, he has cheered this happy gathering. For we is a troubled people—we has lived long with suffering. Brother Hays has made it easier. You see, we has been tossted from center to circumpasses. We has rasst-led on the surface of the restless sea, but we has kept our heads above the drowning waves and tonight we has seen a vision of paradisal glory."

Here was the idea and mood that produced the moving spiritual "Nobody knows de trouble I'se seen, Nobody knows but Jesus," but contemporary events testify that we are beginning to know more about that suffering and it is help-ing us to calm the surface of the restless social sea. I never hear the Negroes sing without having to suppress the impulse to offer a response myself, to interrupt with the assertion, "Oh, yes, we do know and a lot of people are trying to do something about it."

In January, 1925, the ties that bound me happily to my boyhood home were severed by my appointment as assistant attorney general of the state, and my wife and year-old daughter went with me to Little Rock to begin a new kind of professional activity—one that plunged me into political struggles and social pursuits that brought exciting ex-periences.

CHAPTER TWO

From State House to Capitol Hill

MY ARRIVAL IN LITTLE ROCK THIS TIME MEANT AN INTIMATE involvement in the affairs of the city and of the state. As director of the civil law division of Attorney General Applegate's office I was entrusted with litigation affecting the Juvenile Courts, the Commissioner of Labor, the Department of Education, and other agencies having to do with human problems. I was as fascinated by the philosophical and moral aspects of the problems as by the legal. Especially interesting was the duty of advising the State Superintendent of Juvenile Courts. It was a fine outlet for my interest in social work and led to my election later as president of the State Conference of Social Work. It brought me in contact with civic leaders, white and Negro, who were concerned with penal problems, particularly those involving youth.

My family, politics, and church work took a good deal of my time during the State House days, but organized social work kept pulling me into a new orbit, particularly where race problems were involved. My family was sympathetic, my church certainly could not complain, and it was only when political considerations entered the picture that I had to "pay" for indulging a growing concern over the racial minority's aspirations. In that period, I worked chiefly

13

in a non-controversial area. I was interested in better health for Negroes. Tuberculosis, which had claimed my young uncle, a thirty-four-year-old doctor, and several other members of my father's family, had dealt cruelly with the Negro and I found time to work in this field. As president of the Tuberculosis Association I had an opportunity to become acquainted for the first time with leaders of the Negro community—many of them college trained and dedicated people —a reservoir of leadership that the community needed for civic enterprises generally with no relation to race. There is still considerable ignorance among white people of such leadership qualities that might be used for local advancement. There doubtless exists among many of these top-rated Negro leaders a wistfulness for larger outlets, but the needs of their own group are so great that they find themselves preoccupied with programs for Negro welfare with little, if any, thought of how recognition of their talents might come in the white community.

During the twenties when my civic and church activities exposed me to an awareness of the Negro's growing aspiration for an equal legal status with others, I realized that he was steadily acquiring the first essential in a sound program for racial progress, namely, dissatisfaction with his lot and dissatisfaction with the lot of his whole region's position. He was learning in other words that the ceilings that were over him also held down his white neighbor. But his ceiling was even lower and the fact had obvious results in terms of social discontent.

The social workers with whom I was associated in so many enterprises worked hard at the job of equalization. Actually there was complete equality in one important new venture born of the depression—Little Rock's public welfare agency upon whose board of five members I served. We had no tax revenue and no official status. We were selected in a public

mass meeting and had to depend upon voluntary contributions. We were saddened many times by a depleted treasury
but managed to provide something every week for our
families—never making a distinction between white and
Negro. I recall that once I had to approve a weekly allow-
ance for each family of only $1.65 because that was all
there was and we could only hope that government com-
modities would round out a minimum diet for our families.

An outgrowth of my church and civic interracial activity
was the establishment of friendships with Negro ministers
and other Negroes that sometimes achieved a pleasant give-
and-take informality. One was with a Methodist preacher
who called me one Sunday morning to ask if he might attend
the class of men which I taught. I assured him of a cordial
welcome. Later in an intergroup meeting I commented, "It
was certainly gracious for a Negro Methodist minister to
listen to a Bible talk by a white Baptist layman"—only to get
this retort, "Well, of course, there was nothing Methodistic
in your talk; strangely enough, nothing Baptistic, and really
very little of a religious nature." The establishment of such
ties of confidence, enabling the Negro "to be himself," advances mutual understanding and good will and depletes
any false feelings of superiority which the majority group
might display.

White men, in this period of transition, may be unduly
sensitive to articulateness on the Negro's part and, because
of the historic relationship, may resent it; but we would do
well to encourage the naturalness in human relations that
gives the Negro a sense of "belonging." Everything that
builds his sense of dignity is good for his race and for the
progress of both races.

My own insights in the race attitudes were improved by
these contacts. I recall, for example, how I suddenly realized
that I had misunderstood something that the Negro singer

Roland Hayes said about his mother's parting injunction when he left Tennessee to go north. "Always remember," he quoted her as saying, "who you are." I thought at the time that she was warning him not to let any successes destroy humility. Now I think what she meant was, "Remember you're a Hayes and we have family pride and respectability to protect." We of the white majority must not fail to recognize that at the core of the Negroes' aspirations is the firm desire to maintain this family and racial pride—in short, human dignity—and it has little to do with the question of social intermingling.

In 1928, after a year in the private practice of law, I made the race for governor briefly referred to in the opening chapter. My defeat left no scars. There were no racial angles and I guess that fewer than one hundred Negroes in the entire state voted in that primary. In 1930 I made a second race for governor—a furiously fought campaign, but again there were no racial factors. This second defeat hurt me financially but not otherwise. It even laid the basis for my election in the 1932 primary as Democratic national committeeman, a position I held for seven years.

The turning point in my political course came in my candidacy in a 1933 special election for Congress. My record and behavior had angered the political leaders of one county in the district and they found an opportunity to punish me. With a registration of only 1,632 people, they reported 1,850 votes for my opponent, who was the beneficiary rather than the perpetrator of the scheme, and 616 votes for me. A fraud had obviously been practiced. (Outside of that county I had a lead of 595 votes.) It became the subject of a long and tedious lawsuit. Technicalities blocked my efforts for a recount at every stage, and when at last the judge—a sincere, honest man who wanted to correct a wrong that showed on its face—had to dismiss the case because of higher court rulings, I struggled against human reactions that would impair my faith. But my faith in God and in my fellow man survived that bitter experience. It served to give me a further understanding of the difficulties of a minority group in achieving recognition and proper legal safeguards, and it strengthened my dedication to the cause of universal suffrage and honest elections.

In 1934 I received a telephone call from Miss Frances Perkins, Secretary of Labor, that led to my connection with the federal government and eight years of employment in industrial and agricultural programs that again provided outlets for my social welfare interests. Miss Perkins invited me to serve as legal adviser in the Arkansas office of NRA, and I was happy to accept. The agency had a rugged existence and perished with the Supreme Court's "sick chicken" decision, but it had a morale building value for both workers and employers. I learned a good deal about the economic life of the South and the interrelationships that made it necessary for employers to have federal help in meeting sweat-shop competition.

In 1934 lack of wage standards for interstate industries was an evil not only from the point of view of labor but of legitimate employers as well. In my legal service for NRA I found, for example, an Arkansas garment factory employing Negro workers at a weekly wage of $5.00 to $7.00. In the language of one competitor who wanted no exploitation of workers of either race, "That plant is playing havoc with the garment trade from South Carolina to California."

I appealed to the management to pay code wages and struck a balance of back wages due his employees totaling above $5,000. The employees called a meeting to discuss their claim and appointed a spokesman, a Negro woman, to ask my help. I went to the town to explain the law to her, and when I drove up to her little home I heard her say to a

neighbor, "I believe that's my Little Rock lawyer. I'm count-
ing heavy on my Little Rock lawyer. I want to talk to that
Little Rock lawyer, Mr. Brooks Hays." She rushed excitedly
to the car and looked up at me at the wheel. Her face fell
and I suddenly realized that whatever I had in the way of
power to help people, it was not impressive looks. "Good
morning, Mr. Hays," she said, and then turning to her
neighbor, "Of course you know my trust is really in the
Lord."

This was the most dramatic case that I handled for the
government in the collection of wages for Negro workers,
but there were numerous instances in which the wage scale
took a big jump. In spite of the collapse of the blue eagle
agency which had inspired this effort, most of the gains
for the race were preserved in the economic recovery which
was inaugurated in that era.

In May, 1935, I joined the staff of the Resettlement Administration and assisted in the rural rehabilitation program
of that agency and its successors. In this capacity I learned
at first hand something of the Negro farmers' difficulties. The
white farmers were in trouble, too, but while one in three
of the white farmers owned their land, only one in five of
the Negro farmers were owners. Farm tenancy was an evil
that plagued the nation's agricultural leadership of that
period, but substantial headway was made in a legislative
charting of the solution under the terms of the Bankhead–
Jones Act of 1937 which set up liberal credit facilities to
enable tenants to acquire land and owners to operate farms.

While the community project, the so-called model farm
colonies, received more publicity than the less exciting type
of rehabilitation sponsored by Resettlement, it was my
opinion that the credit facilities and the supervised farm
and home program for individual farmers "in place" was

the most significant part of our work, particularly for the Negro farmer.

Farm Security's (Resettlement's later name) value was not accurately measured by income statistics. Better food, more tastefully cooked and preserved, on pantry shelves and better dresses for the farm girls reflected the fact that social returns accompanied the improved "business" arrangements for the farmer. The pressure cookers had a part to play in home management plans and our home supervisors were not just quipping when they called them "the precious cookers."

The rehabilitation program became an intimate part of the family's tie to the government. This is well illustrated by the answer of a Negro pupil to a question propounded to the primary grade in a small country school in Arkansas. "Who is the President of the United States?" the teacher asked. No one answered. Finally one child raised his hand. "Miss Myrtle," he said, "I don't know who the President is, but Mr. Hanna is our Farm Security supervisor."

As I now recall my thought processes in this period I gave little thought to the Negro's ambition for immediate participation in the elections. I was confident that in time he would be admitted to a larger share of the region's economic and political life, but the *educational* preparation for that looked like a task big enough to engage those of us who were particularly concerned about his health and well-being —and by education I was thinking of the mental conditioning of the whites as well as advancement in learning for the Negro. I viewed the problem largely in terms of winning concessions in the way of opportunities for him—higher wages, better schools and housing, and a quickened but noncontroversial stepping up of his progress. It was during that time that I acted as spokesman for the Urban League, whose Little Rock chapter I had helped organize, in appealing to the mayor to employ some Negro policemen in Negro districts. I was turned down primarily because white patrolmen strongly opposed the idea. Again, that attitude was changed and Negro police, carefully selected and trained, are today a part of the enforcement machinery. The plan has worked well in Little Rock and other Southern cities and is rapidly being adopted in the larger communities.

I felt honored to be asked in 1937 to become a member of the Commission on Interracial Cooperation, a non-governmental association of representatives of both races financed largely by the Rosenwald Foundation and headed by Will W. Alexander, whose dedication to improving the status of Negroes made him one of the South's distinguished figures. I met him first when he headed the Farm Security Administration, and for a while I served as his assistant. Many worthwhile interracial activities of the period were traceable to the Commission and to Will Alexander's imaginative and devoted leadership. Some efforts did not bear fruit at once and it was because of the conservative approach of the Commission that a few Negroes were critical and sought more militant outlets. But it is evident now that ideas generated by the Commission and promoted in localities throughout the South did have an impact.

To understand that impact, it is necessary to take a backward glance and a quick appraisal of some of the changes. I was close enough to the severe economic struggles of Little Rock Negroes during the thirties to grasp the significance of the tremendous progress enjoyed by the group as a whole in recent years. Their new purchasing power has brought concessions to their effort to remove all signs of a subordinate status. Take, for example, the signs over drinking fountains in public places "For White" and "For Colored." Many of them have been removed in department stores, and it has been accomplished quietly by Negro committees representing customers who were embarrassed by them. In the old days, customer pressure would not have accomplished it. It reflects the prestige of customers who were entitled on the basis of a new patronage to urge their own point of view upon the store management. In the meantime their fellow white customers were coming to realize that justice and fair play required some changes.

In 1938 I advocated repeal of Arkansas' poll-tax requirement for voting. It was primarily a question of political morals as I viewed it. I wanted to knock out block purchases of poll-tax receipts by those with a selfish interest to serve and to make it easier for the rank and file to qualify for voting. The political machines always prefer complicated ways of getting names on the voting list. This is not to discount altogether the significance of a barrier for the low-income population of both races—$1.00 ($1.50 or $2.00 in some states) was a bigger item in the average family budget of the thirties than it is today.

A letter I received from President Roosevelt on this subject aroused a good deal of interest and is worth reproducing at this time:

Hyde Park, New York
September 9, 1938

Mr. Brooks Hays
Democratic National Committeeman
Little Rock, Arkansas

Dear Brooks:

Thank you for your interesting letter about the proposal to repeal the poll tax.

I think we should all remember that free suffrage has come in almost every state after a long struggle. At the time of the adoption of the federal constitution some form of property qualification was a prerequisite for voting—and in some states this amounted to a denial of the privilege of voting to a large proportion of the adult male population of the state.

Gradually, through the years, state after state abolished the requirement of owning real estate, or of owning an equivalent amount of some other kind of property. Then came efforts to restrict the franchise by the imposition of poll taxes.

I am glad to know that there is such a general move in those states which still have them to repeal them altogether. They are inevitably contrary to the fundamental democracy and its representative form of government in which we believe.

The imposition of a poll tax which prevents a large number of otherwise qualified men and women from voting is not far removed from the effort of some people in the state of Maine two years ago to prevent men and women who, through no fault of their own, were receiving relief from voting because of an old law that denied the vote to people in poor houses.

I am, of course, not advising the voters of the state of Arkansas how to vote on this question—but there is no reason under the sun why I should not talk about an important general principle that applies under our constitutional form of government in every state in the union.

Very sincerely yours,
(signed) Franklin D. Roosevelt

This letter from the President focused national interest on the movement to abolish the Arkansas poll tax. The proposal failed, as have subsequent efforts to remove the tax as a voting requirement. Any good that we may have accomplished in acquainting the people with the disadvantages of the tax has been offset by their understandable resentment of efforts to force removal by federal action. Mr. Roosevelt's tactful reference to the right of states to determine policy should have set the pattern, but it was disregarded. The strategy of resort to federal action was a mistake which many of us who had helped pioneer the movement in the South vigorously opposed.

The advocacy of reforms in election machinery was one of many interests which engaged my energies as Democratic national committeeman. During this period I did considerable traveling in Southern states and made a few speeches in the interest of interracial cooperation. The one time that I met Margaret Mitchell, the author, I was impressed by her deep understanding and appreciation of the Negro people. I was in Atlanta attending a Southern Policy Conference and was invited to a tea in her honor. It was at the time when Hollywood's machinery for filming *Gone With The Wind* was getting underway, and everyone was discussing the casting of the principal characters. I was chatting with the hostess and a small, attractive woman while we waited, as I thought, for Miss Mitchell. I was probably the only person in Little Rock who had not read the book; but having an ingrained dislike for letting a conversation pass me by, I was just opening my mouth to say so, in a bragging spirit, when the small woman—not my hostess—said, "I don't care whom they select for Scarlet or Rhett, but I do care about my Negroes. I want actors who will give them dignity. They must have *dignity.*" It was Margaret Mitchell! After I had recovered from the shock of the *faux pas* I had nearly made, I was able to appreciate and admire her attitude.

My departure from the Department of Agriculture in 1942 was inspired by my faith in my ability to win the seat in Congress that I had unsuccessfully sought in 1933. My hopes were fulfilled, but only after a last-minute desperate effort by my opponent, the Lieutenant Governor of Arkansas, to exploit the race situation. My most effective answer was the citation of a resolution adopted the previous year by the Methodist women. It obviously was designed to meet just the type of campaigning in which my opponent was indulging:

"We recommend that, as one of our obligations as Christian citizens, we educate against the injection of race as an issue in political campaigns;

"We further urge the women of the Southeastern Jurisdiction to use all their powers against this practice."

Quoted also was the statement prepared by request of the secretary of the Christian Social Relations and Local Church Activities, Southeastern Jurisdiction, Woman's Society of Christian Service, the Methodist Church:

"Race as an issue is the refuge of demagogs who as candidates must divert attention from their own records and from the greed of special interests supporting them for office."

The good faith efforts to foster improved race relations had borne fruit!

CHAPTER THREE

Civil Rights and the Arkansas Plan

As a new member of the House in 1943 I learned that I had a reputation to live down in the eyes of some of the senior Southerners. I could not renounce my moderate liberalism but, being what one North Carolina friend termed a "states' rights liberal," I felt that I was entitled to membership in "the lodge." I wanted to feel at ease in the cloakroom with the Southern members. Perhaps they did not know that in the famous Birmingham Conference on Human Welfare in 1939 and in other regional meetings I had opposed a move to appeal to Congress to outlaw poll taxes. I explained to them, as I had previously explained to Northern liberals, that while I had sponsored the repeal proposal in Arkansas by state action, I opposed federal intervention in this matter. My maiden speech six months after I took office made my position clear on this point. That talk cancelled out to some extent the impression that my service in "Rex Tugwell's agency" had created among some. I deplored the agitation for dealing with the region's problems through ill-advised and hastily conceived national legislation based on "the liberal line." The Northern liberals were making more difficult the role of Southern progressives who wanted real progress through the educational and political facilities of the respective states. They were plunging us toward a crisis in the region that would create bitterness and strife.

For a while after that speech, my conversations with these Southern colleagues (whose good will was indispensable if I were to become influential) sounded like one I once heard my father describe. Father asked a neighboring farmer, "What were you and Mr. Blevins talking about so heatedly?" and he replied, "Well, he said to me, 'Ed, I believe the watermelons grow best in the sandy land,' and I said, 'That's what I think, too,' so we argued it out right there."

As an indication of the general spirit of Congress at that time, regarding matters of race, it is worth recalling that when William L. Dawson of Chicago, the only Negro member of Congress at that time, received his oath of office the same month that I did, January, 1943, a group of Georgia congressmen went to his office to welcome one of their native sons to the House of Representatives. It was an unusual courtesy and Mr. Dawson was deeply moved by the experience. He told me about it himself. The highly respected Carl Vinson spoke for the group and assured the new member that the people of Georgia were proud that "one of their boys had received this great honor."

In the conversation in which this was related the congressman told me some of his early experiences as a Pullman porter. He showed a better understanding of some of the South's social complexities than some who have not lived in the region. He told me of a trip into the South on a Pullman assignment in company with another porter not acquainted with the region. In a deep South community the train was delayed a long time and the two porters had the problem of getting something to eat. The grocery stores were closed. The only cafe in town refused to feed "colored." They walked back and sat down dejectedly by their cars. The other porter was bitter. Dawson pleaded with him to be patient. "These people are OK," he said. "You wait." A little boy came along and Dawson hailed him. "Please tell your mother," he said, "that there are two poor old colored men over here who are hungry and we will pay her for something to eat." In a few minutes he was back with sandwiches and pie, but when Dawson asked, "How much?" he replied, "Mama said she wouldn't think of letting you pay anything and she was glad to do it."

"Now, you see," said the new congressman, "we'd rather have had it done the other way but if anyone assumes that the objectionable customs are due to lack of generosity and human kindness on the part of white people they don't know the South. I like to remember that lady's kindness rather than the closed door of the cafe which, though unjust, was after all impersonal. Things are changing and when enough people like that lady study and see things in their true perspective they'll change faster."

I asked Mr. Dawson, "Do you think Southern white people understand the Negro better than his new neighbors?" He was thoughtful. "They should," he finally said, "but don't forget that he understands both of you better than either of you understands him." I pondered that one. "You see," he added, "he studies you—he has to—and while he does you are busy running the business of the country—and the government." This study of the reaction of his white brethren to the appeal for civil rights was to lead Mr. Dawson to stronger assertions in behalf of his fellow Negroes, but it never caused him to lose perspective on the problems to be overcome or on the progress being made.

It was not until V-E Day approached that Congress found much time for the proposals advanced in behalf of minorities, the so-called civil rights bills. During World War II, President Roosevelt had established a federal Fair Employment Practices Commission, which was regarded by liberals and by minority groups as an essential new piece of administrative machinery. No longer were we to permit the waste of human resources because of intolerance, prejudice, or bigotry. In the post-war world, after the Nazi Aryan concept had been smashed, we would give greater emphasis than before to the equality of men and the Bill of Rights. For those concerned with the problem of civil rights, FEPC was regarded as a symbol of the brave new world.

Other issues were swept into prominence at that time, including a renewed cry for strong penalties in cases of lynching, increasing demands for the abolition of the poll tax, and rising indignation against such Jim Crow practices as segregated travel in interstate commerce. It is significant to note that these issues provided the major battleground of the 1940's, rather than the right to vote or segregation in the schools—although the latter were given some attention, of course. It seems characteristic of a broad social problem such as race relations that the minority group tends to focus on certain areas for certain periods of time and then to shift its attention to other areas. The cycle continues, however, and old issues, if not resolved, have a way of returning to the forefront of public attention.

On the subject of the FEPC I had an opportunity to present my viewpoint during the spring of 1945 when Congressman Charles M. LaFollette of Indiana agreed to debate with me the provisions of a bill proposing the creation of a permanent Fair Employment Practices Commission. It was our intention to demonstrate to the House that this emotion-charged issue could be debated with temperateness and a mutual acknowledgment of good faith. We were granted time for a discussion of this proposal on April 23, 1945. Mr. LaFollette was one of the sponsors of a permanent FEPC, while I was known to oppose this particular piece of legislation. By dividing the allotted time equally, with opportunity for rebuttal, we were confident that we could present the best possible case for the positions we held. In order to avoid being sidetracked, we declined to yield for interruptions which might have stirred up the acrimony customarily associated with the issue.

Mr. LaFollette began the debate by stating his belief that the bill was designed "to extend the ethic upon which this country is established and in which we profess to believe, into the field of economic life." He realized that no legislation could eliminate prejudice. While he acknowledged that prejudice is something "which sits inside of people," he felt that the federal government could eliminate the outward effect of prejudice which is discrimination. As far as the basic human feelings and desires are concerned, he left the necessary changes to the process of education. Even in this area, however, he was optimistic about the value of legislation, revealing that he was of the opinion, shared by many others, that "there is educational value inherent in the enforcement provisions of this legislation, that people will come close together when they know there is behind a federal agency a power eventually to enforce action to prohibit discrimination."

My answer began with a reference to "the points on which we agree, and they are as important as those on which we differ." I continued, "We both believe that we must do everything that men in positions of political responsibility can do to preserve the democratic means of settling differences between groups. I hope that when action on the bill is concluded the victors will not say, 'Now that settles it— we have downed them.' This is the sort of problem that requires continuous and intelligent study. If the bill should be defeated, I will be relieved, for, from my point of view, a threat to important governmental principles will be removed, but a victory should be followed by cooperation in those things that will assure minority workers of just and equitable treatment."

My opposition was due not to indifference to discrimination but rather to my belief that the problem of fair employment should be approached from the viewpoint of local acceptance. It was in this spirit that I said, "Government cannot supply the motive for unity; it can only supply the mechanics, and if the motive is lacking, no governmental process will succeed." It was my contention that until a greater degree of public support could be marshaled for enforcement of such a law it would crash, as some other federal measures have, upon the rock of popular resistance. I pointed out my lifetime interest in the problems of underprivileged people, particularly my efforts on behalf of better race relations, and then attempted to show how my attitude toward this legislation was consistent with that position. It was my firm belief that "what the Negro really needs in the realm of civic and economic life, as distinguished from social pursuits, is the lessening of his race connection. How, then, in the name of simple logic, can anyone expect to help him with this bill? It would accentuate the race tie and would set in motion counter movements to retard him."

I felt that I spoke for a great multitude of conscientious and sincere Southerners who were searching for solutions to the difficulties of the minority group that did not do violence to the authentic traditions and deep-rooted values of the region. I said then, "We are not bitter over the evidences of outside interest in our problem, for that problem affects the political life of the North and the West. The problem is not exclusively ours. It has a national, indeed in some respects an international, character. Colored people of other countries have been told that America will not treat her colored minorities properly. That is disturbing, and I trust that when the whole story is told—when our minority citizens appraise the genuine forces for justice at work in this country—they will interpret our actions correctly. We owe it to them to take this action without rancor and with proper regard for new world conditions. We could not repress these human concerns if we would. Our own sympathies are expansive. We are interested in disadvantaged peoples, too—even those of other continents—and we know that this quality in human life defies geography."

While paying tribute to the sound advice given their brethren by many Negro leaders, I pointed out that certain self-appointed spokesmen for the race had denounced the best friends the Negro has among the white people. They had succeeded temporarily in marring the spirit of good will and confidence that had existed between liberal white leadership and the Negroes of our region. They were willing to subject their race to the bitterness and distrust that must inevitably follow that course, although extremely few of them lived in the South where estrangement might affect the daily lives of Negroes. I expressed the determination "to do everything I can to change that trend and to help establish or rather to restore those contacts between the races that make for the constructive improvements of both." I conceded, of course, that responsibility for inadequate contacts between the races rested upon both.

My friendly opponent generously helped me circulate my views, and we were pleased with the response. Some evidence of our success was the number of requests that came in for copies of our speeches from all parts of the country. Young people in particular seemed interested in the fact that there had been a formal debate that was free from bitterness and recrimination. It was this fact rather than any profound contributions we made to the subject matter that attracted attention. Several columnists commented on its significance from that standpoint. We were asked to repeat the performance before groups outside Washington, but as I recall it we were able to accept only one of these invitations which came from a policy committee in Philadelphia. Made up largely of liberals, it inclined to the views of Mr. LaFollette rather than my middle-of-the-road position, but the group was interested in the fact that there was something besides a politically orthodox viewpoint in my presentation.

This debate was significant in that it made clear that Congress could be a meeting ground for men of good will of all regions, and it demonstrated the desire to analyze and attempt to work out suitable solutions for the problems of minority groups. It was my hope that I could serve as one of the spokesmen in the House of Representatives for the moderate South which was anxious to adapt to the changing times, provided regional patterns of life were not violently torn apart. The nation had to be shown that the Southern extremists were not any more representative of the region than the Northern extremists were of the North.

With the question of civil rights still uppermost in the minds of many Americans, there was a growing desire for information on exactly what the status of minority rights was in the United States. Many proposals and counter-proposals had been made, but the actual facts of the situation were unknown. In recognition of this need President Truman issued Executive Order 9808 on December 5, 1946, establishing the President's Committee on Civil Rights, with a mandate to "inquire into and determine whether and in what respect current law-enforcement measures and the authority and means possessed by Federal, State and local governments may be strengthened and improved to safeguard the civil rights of the people ... and make recommendations [to the President] with respect to the adoption or establishment, by legislation or otherwise, of more adequate and effective means and procedures for the protection of the civil rights of the people of the United States."

When the Civil Rights Commission issued its report in 1947, a bitter controversy was inspired which threatened to destroy whatever good will Mr. LaFollette and I had fostered. President Truman seemed to embrace all of its recommendations, and he stirred up a political fight in the South exceeding in intensity anything that had happened since the Reconstruction period. I felt at the time that our reaction was too emotional and that real progress in the field of improved race relations and a wider extension of basic rights could not be made until tempers cooled and a degree of objectivity could be achieved.

Incidentally, one important point generally overlooked is that the President did not actually approve all of the Commission's recommendations, and his refusal to go along with the more extreme proposals—as, for example, suggestions that federal aid of various types be withheld in states not meeting certain civil rights standards laid down in the Commission's statement—reflected greater understanding of the South's position than Mr. Truman generally gets credit for. I believe there were other phases of the report that failed to receive his sanction. It would be interesting if Mr. Truman would elaborate upon the known fact that he did not transmit these suggestions to the Congress with his personal approval. It is well known, of course, that he was officially adamant and, while he saw me on two occasions in 1949 to discuss ideas I had on the subject, he conceded nothing. There was some significance in the fact that, while on the occasion of our first talk I was ushered through a back door and the newspaper men were not told I was seeing the President, on my second visit I was on the official guest list and was interviewed when I came out of his office. About all I told the newsmen was that I had discussed civil rights with the President and that, while he was friendly and interested in my efforts to compose the differences, he did not agree with me. I made it clear to the newspapermen that I had not convinced him of the merits of my approach. Yet I may have convinced him that if we ever get anywhere with federal legislation it will be along these lines. If the President had had only civil rights to deal with and if he had been a little more familiar with the intricacies of Southern social problems, I think he might have been able to take up my plan (soon to be discussed) without compromising his position or losing face with the civil rights group.

It was unfortunate that, in choosing the Commission, Mr. Truman failed to give to the Southern states a larger representation and to include among the region's representatives some who had more conventional views than the two very admirable people, Frank Graham of North Carolina and Mrs. M. E. Tilly of Georgia, entertained. Just as Mr. Truman might have some enlightening comments on the differences which he had with the Commission, Frank Graham could give detailed points of difference between himself and the Commission majority. He was familiar enough with the practical difficulties in the way of accomplishing many of the goals to realize that legislatively some of the recommendations were not realistic. It was regrettable that he did not find time to file a minority report, for the record does not reveal that he dissented from some of the major recommendations, though I know that in some respects these recommendations did not have his approval.

Malcolm Ross, chairman of the war-time FEPC, included several open letters to "Southern liberals," challenging their position on the establishment of a permanent FEPC in a book he wrote on his regulatory experience, entitled *All Manner of Men.* The following was his letter to me:

The Hon. Brooks Hays
United States House of Representatives
Washington, D.C.

Dear Congressman:

I'm sorry we never got around to that longer talk on FEPC we promised each other last time I saw you briefly at the Capitol. I wanted to tell you that I thought your debate with Charlie LaFollette was a fine thing to do. You two started a precedent by arguing the race question wihout rancor. You and Charlie certainly left by the same South and North doors by which you entered, but that calm give-and-take debate was a landmark, and I think it will someday persuade others to stop ranting and put their heads together on this thing.

Of course I think that the Indiana redhead was right and you wrong in your conclusions on the workability of a federal law against discrimination. My reasons are summed up in the book which (necessarily) accompanies this letter.

There is one statement of yours which I'd like to discuss specifically. You said: "It is unity of purpose we seek, not enforced relationships." That sounds better than it really is. Look, unity of purpose is what the South and the North desperately need. But "enforced relationships" is too broad a term to describe what would happen if minority-group workers were given their chance of promotion in Southern industry. . . .

I hope you will not be offended if I point out that a criticism of enforced relationships is not a tenable Southern position. There are in this country no more striking examples of enforced relationships than those imposed on Southern Negroes by white supremacy and on Mexican-Americans by its Anglo version.

None of your arguments against federal intervention make cheap use of "social equality" and other terror-inspiring catchwords which some of your colleagues have done to death. But

I imagine that it is just that bitter resentment at outside interference which you fear may be aggravated by any federal attempt, no matter how well intentioned. I also see that danger, and I think it can only be overcome by a Southern realization that enforced equality of job opportunity is the mildest possible restriction. It touches only something which everyone recognizes as an evil. It leaves all the other race relations alone, and relies solely on the economic betterment of Negroes and Mexican-Americans to work its slow but sure curative process on present race animosities. . . .

Sincerely,
Malcolm Ross

His challenge encouraged me to give long and serious thought to the problem of presenting an alternative plan acceptable to the North and compatible with the best interests of the South. Such a program would, of course, have to be based on the recognition by the moderates that opposition to federal controls rested on the nature of federal and state powers. While many other issues have a clear national focus, a central Washington office could not possibly handle justly the local situations that would arise under a compulsory FEPC law. It was from this perspective that I hoped to formulate proposals that would not do violence to either the standards of equal justice or the value systems of any region.

I was still trying to find an acceptable middle-ground between the Truman position and that of some of my Southern brethren when the 1948 political campaigns began. My contribution to the National Democratic party stand on civil rights was really to begin after the 1948 Democratic Convention, but I attended that Convention to see whether the party could work out a satisfactory compromise. It was my deep concern over the split that occurred between the North and the South, leading to the Dixiecrat movement, that caused me to take a more active part in later Congressional debates and led me to enter the civil rights platform-writing picture in the 1952 and 1956 conventions.

Even before the Convention began on July 12, 1948, there were evidences of a great chasm between the different factions of the party. President Harry Truman, hoping to be renominated, was faced with movements on the Left and on the Right to dump him from the ticket in order to strengthen the chances for a Democratic victory in November. Mr. Truman was anxious to preserve unity and remain the standard-bearer at the head of the ticket. The White House reportedly sent a draft of what it would consider an acceptable platform to the eighteen-member platform subcommittee, set up to prepare a preliminary statement for the consideration of the full 108-member Platform Committee. This draft was assumed to contain a civil rights section which would not do violence to the position of the South, already aroused by the Report of the President's Civil Rights Commission and by his message to the Congress on February 2, 1948, advocating specific legislative objectives in the civil rights area. President Truman was trying to hold the Northern liberals "in line" while he moved to regain the confidence of Southern conservatives and states' rights advocates. His chances for success in this field appeared dim, even when his own renomination became assured following the refusal of General Eisenhower to accept the call of the Americans for Democratic Action to run for president and the failure of the Southerners to find an effective alternative candidate to rally around in their efforts to unseat him.

J. Howard McGrath, Chairman of the Democratic National Committee at that time, expected an open fight on the civil rights plank, but he hoped to keep it within bounds by repeating the language of the 1944 plank. The important passages of that statement read as follows:

"We believe that the country which has the greatest measure of social justice is capable of the greatest achievements.

"We believe that racial and religious minorities have the right to live, develop and vote equally with all citizens and share the rights that are guaranteed by our Constitution. Congress should exert its full constitutional powers to protect those rights."

He had not figured on the crusading impulses of Mayor Hubert Humphrey of Minneapolis, a member of the preliminary drafting body. The young mayor revealed, however, that he would fight in committee for the inclusion in the platform of all ten points of President Truman's civil rights program. Mayor Humphrey assured his associates that, if he lost his contest, he would file a minority report, carrying the whole issue to the floor of the Convention. His minimum demand was the inclusion of pledges covering at least four of the civil rights recommendations, namely: (a) abolition of poll taxes as a condition of voting for federal officials; (b) a federal anti-lynching law; (c) a Fair Employment Practices Commission, and (d) non-segregation of races in the Armed Forces.

When the Convention began on Monday, the special seven-member preliminary drafting body sought for the harmony necessary to see the document through the two other platform groups (18-member and 108-member) and the Convention itself. It was now clear that the platform, and especially the civil rights section, would be the "last stand" of the South. Many Southern conservatives opposed even the mild 1944 plank on the grounds that it served as the "foundation" of President Truman's civil rights program. In defiance of Mayor Humphrey, they went so far as to reject a mere repetition of the 1944 clauses and threatened to introduce their own floor amendments, demanding a pledge for the preservation of states' rights. (The wording of this amendment was intended to be so strict that Congress would have to construe it as barring federal intervention even with aid funds.) While no realistic Southerner expected to get such a proposal adopted, the strategy was to scare enough state delegations into supporting a more moderate compromise.

When the seven-member group submitted its report to the eighteen-member writing committee, the document came under assault from all directions. Here is how it read:

The Democratic party and the Democratic administrations are solely responsible for the great gains in recent years made in the continuing efforts to reduce and eliminate unfair and illegal discrimination based on race, creed, or color.

We have implemented our often-expressed belief that racial and religious minorities had the right to live, develop, and vote equally with all citizens and to share the rights guaranteed by the Constitution.

We again call on Congress to exercise full authority to the limits of its Constitutional powers to protect these rights.

A quick examination revealed this to be a virtual rewriting of the compromise of 1944. While Southern Democrats denounced it as unacceptable, Northern Democrats declared it to be so weak that they were ready to battle against it. Despite these howls of protest, the more reasonable liberals were preparing to head off any floor fight from their direction, also arguing backstage that if the Southerners started such a fight, they could be voted down promptly and the platform could then be rushed through to Convention approval. Some ardent liberals continued to argue that the civil rights plank should be made stronger and that it should "put the issues on the line."

The eighteen-member subcommittee at first accepted a mild clause upholding states' rights, but eventually struck this clause from the civil rights section. As the more ardent liberals of the North and West gradually gained dominance in the Committee, the plank was altered in minor ways to conform with the original Humphrey–ADA statement. Humphrey then won his greatest battle when the Committee agreed to include demands for specific federal action (principally Congressional) on such issues as poll taxes, lynching, employment practices where racial questions were involved, and segregation within the Armed Forces. As the civil rights draft went to the full resolutions body for final recommendation, the stronger plank was put up for approval. The South had not yet given up and now prepared a major effort for revision before the document reached the Convention floor.

Democratic party leaders acting on behalf of the President were successful in getting the full 108-member Platform Committee to reverse its subcommittee's stand and reject Humphrey's program. They thereby hoped to mollify the South, and thus they brought before the delegates a civil rights platform pledge which was restricted to the generalities sought by the moderates. Everything depended now on quick Convention acceptance of this new compromise.

Now an unexpected dramatic development changed the course of events and led to disaster. Former Governor Dan Moody of Texas introduced an amendment from the floor calling for party support of states' rights. (Another similar amendment was offered by Cecil Sims, delegate of Tennessee.) All the work of the moderates went up in smoke! Although fourteen other delegates from eight of the eleven Southern states sponsored this amendment, the general reception to their pleas foretold impending defeat. When the moderates then called for support of the platform as submitted, they were met by demands for "even stronger stuff." The Southern demands for a states' rights plan were overwhelmingly rejected by a vote of 925 to 309. As a Tennessean remarked, "They over-egged their pudding."

In the face of the Southern argument that the upholding or throwing down of the Constitution itself was at stake in this platform, the Northern liberals proceeded to demonstrate wildly for the acceptance of the strongly worded Humphrey amendment. Humphrey himself led a ten-minute demonstration and then spoke to the delegates as follows: "We are 172 years late in acting. It is now time for the Democratic party to get out of the shadow of states' rights and walk forthrightly in the bright sunshine of human rights, march down the high road of progressive democracy." Backed by Andrew Biemiller of Wisconsin, Mrs. Esther Murray of California, and Aaron L. Jacoby of New York (and generally supported by old-time New Dealers and urban liberals), he won his floor fight for a plank with real teeth in it, by the narrow margin of 651½ to 582½. Party harmony was destroyed and the voice of moderation lost in the roars.

The adoption of the entire platform then came by voice vote. The South was through as an effective influence in shaping the work and results of the Convention. Here is the platform as it was finally adopted by the delegates:

The Democratic Party is responsible for the great civil rights gains made in recent years in eliminating unfair and illegal discrimination based on race, creed or color.

The Democratic Party commits itself to continuing its efforts to eradicate all racial, religious, and economic discrimination.

We again state our belief that racial and religious minorities must have the right to live, the right to work, the right to vote, the full and equal protection of the laws, on a basis of equality with all citizens as guaranteed by the Constitution.

We highly commend President Harry S. Truman for his courageous stand on the issue of civil rights. We call upon Congress to

support our President in guaranteeing these basic and fundamental American principles:

(1) The right of full and equal political participation;
(2) The right to equal opportunity of employment;
(3) The right of security of person;
(4) The right of equal treatment in the service and
    defense of our nation.

While the men who started the uproar, Governor Moody
and Mr. Sims, accepted the verdict of the Convention at the
time it was declared, other Southerners were outraged. Half
of the delegation of Alabama, the first state on the roll call,
and the full Mississippi delegation had prepared carefully
for this moment. They intended to obtain recognition from
the chairman, state their objections to the platform, and
then walk dramatically from the Convention Hall. In this
they were foiled by a fellow Southerner, Chairman of the
Convention Sam Rayburn, who, well aware of what was
afoot, broke the maneuver by refusing to consider any proposal other than to recess.

These delegates did walk out after the recess was over,
but the impact of their maneuver was greatly diminished.
The other Southerners stayed on, even when their last
protest candidate for president, Governor Laney of Arkansas,
withdrew his candidacy because he could not accept the
platform. President Truman was renominated soon thereafter and the Dixiecrat movement was on its way to forma-
tion in the South. Thus it was that intransigence on both
sides (*not* fostered by party leaders) led to this unfortunate
crisis in the long-run fortunes of the Democratic party.

The capture of many Southern states for the Republican
candidate in 1956, in spite of Mr. Eisenhower's position and
his party's position on civil rights, reveals that much of the
opposition to Mr. Truman in 1948 was attributable not to

the civil rights issue but to economic cleavages that had been slowly developing in the region. I recall telling Mr. Truman shortly after the 1948 election that his civil rights position was responsible for only a fraction of the disaffected vote. He laughed heartily over the story I gave him to illustrate it: A couple invited their neighbors to dinner. It was a sumptuous meal and the guests were quite impressed. One inquired of the host, "How long has your cook been with you?" He replied, "She never was with us. She was against us from the start."

In spite of the Dixiecrat movement, Mr. Truman won re-election and continued his efforts to have civil rights legislation enacted. It seems likely that much of his strength came from Northern minority groups who rewarded his championing of their cause by returning him to the White House. These groups, however, did not have control of the influential positions in Congress, still held mostly by Southerners, and we faced open warfare between the executive and legislative branches. I was determined to do everything possible to bring the two wings of the Democratic party together again in the interest of the public welfare. First, I studied the report of the Civil Rights Commission and the President's message to Congress to see what areas of general agreement or possible compromise I might find.

Next, and most important, I made my first speech on the subject in the House on February 2, 1949, just one year after Mr. Truman's submission of his recommendations. I had prepared rather carefully an outline of a legislative program which seemed to represent real progress. I pointed out that not one of the President's major recommendations had been approved and that it seemed appropriate to take a second look both at the President's message and the report of the Commission on Civil Rights upon which the message was based. "The proponents of the civil rights program would surely concede that failure to win Congressional approval of a single item signifies that there are valid and substantial objections to that program. At the same time, as one who has joined generally in the resistance, I am prepared to concede that there are some meritorious features in the report. Furthermore, I concede that the continued agitation for these proposals should be convincing on one point, namely, that the problems do exist, but it should be just as clear that they do not yield to categorical solutions."

I then tried to demonstrate that many of the Commission's recommendations had to do with social aspirations rather than civil rights, and while these were worthy of attention, they were essentially outside the legal or political area. I proposed a series of compromise programs, based upon the maximum concessions each side could make without the sacrifice of basic principles. This legislative program was specific and met the criteria of (1) what was attainable, and (2) what was right. Since the civil rights report dealt with four major controversial matters, segregation in the Armed Services, poll-tax repeal, anti-lynching legislation, and the FEPC, I addressed myself to these four issues as follows:

1. *Segregation in the Armed Services.* While the complete abolition of segregation was probably the ultimate aim of the Negro, it was my belief at this time that it was legislatively the least important. Court decisions and executive orders were accomplishing about all that could be accomplished under the then-prevailing conditions. The United States Supreme Court decision holding that only a policy of non-segregation in interstate transportation conformed to the federal Constitution just about settled that question and I felt that a federal law requiring non-segregation in travel would add nothing to the substantive rights already established. The integration policy adopted first by the

Navy, and then by other branches of the Armed Services, tended to advance the Negro toward his goal. Congress appeared willing to transfer the controversy to the Armed Services, and wise heads on both sides of the civil rights controversy could generally be counted on to avoid spelling out in legislation the course that the Executive should take with reference to segregation in the services. No legislation in this area needed to be recommended for the immediate future. My approach was based on the gains already made by Court decisions and my conviction that under the Constitution the question of segregation was largely a state matter.

For awhile, however, the opponents of segregation insisted on attaching riders to various bills making mandatory complete integration in the Armed Services, though they were never successful. Later, when some of the rulings in the Armed Services seemed to disregard regional patterns, an effort was made to put certain limits on the military, but just as the opponents of segregation failed, so those who tried to compel the Armed Services to restrict non-segregation policies failed in their efforts. The controversy was provoked, perhaps, by the Air Force ruling that no Southern college practicing segregation could participate in certain types of training. It was to meet this situation that Congressman Winstead offered what might be called an anti-integration amendment, though it was destined to fail just as the anti-segregation amendments had failed. Mr. Winstead's approach was based on the idea that a man drafted from a state having segregation laws should be permitted to serve with segregated units if he so desired, but his opponents made the most of precedents for leaving these matters to the services. Except for the Winstead amendment debate and that produced by some amendments offered by John Bell Williams of Mississippi, there was little Congressional discussion of basic segregation policies, and while we all recognized that this matter would continue to be one of the focal points in the controversy, it did not present difficulties at the federal level.

2. *Prohibition of the Poll Tax as a Voting Prerequisite.* It was necessary to deal with this question, since there seemed to be considerable interest in it across the country and proponents of abolishing the tax had been fairly successful in convincing the people outside of poll-tax states that it constituted an unjustifiable obstruction to the franchise. My suggestion, therefore, was that a Constitutional amendment be agreed upon as a part of a one-package compromise, and that the poll-tax states cooperate to the extent of getting the machinery in action for a federal amendment prohibiting the use of the tax as a qualification for voting. Agitation for Congressional action prohibiting the poll tax began about 1938, and always ran into a filibuster in the Senate if pressed by its advocates. It could generally get through the House. With only six states still retaining the poll tax, I had no doubt I could get agreement on this point, although until something in the way of a compromise was agreed upon with reference to the more complicated questions, I knew it would be used as a symbol for Southern resistance. One point often overlooked is that even conservative representatives like Burr Harrison of Virginia agreed to go along with a Constitutional amendment to do away with it, and Mr. Harrison thought it would be much better for us to agree upon this course of action and actually accomplish its abolishment through Constitutional amendment than to take the chance that a Congressional statute outlawing the tax might become a precedent for further federal intervention in election machinery.

3. *Anti-Lynching.* On this question I worked out a rather novel approach, believing that the plan embodied in my anti-lynching bill would be acceptable to those who had a

legitimate fear of federal prosecution of alleged lynchers as well as those who were seeking to protect the rights of accused persons. This was one part of the 1947 civil rights report that dealt strictly with an individual and civil rights, as distinguished from the social aspirations of minority groups.

Incidentally, one of the best letters I received commenting on my proposal came from Mark Ethridge of the *Louisville Courier-Journal*. He was strong for anti-lynching legislation by the Congress and would probably have favored a straight federal statute without the qualifying provisions which my proposal contained. At the same time, students of the lynching evil, such as George S. Mitchell of the Southern Regional Council, believed that my approach, which left primary responsibility for enforcement in the states and projected federal authority only in those situations where prescribed criteria were not met and where the states did not act, would be more effective than a straight federal statute.

I realized that the question of constitutionality was debatable.

The bill provided that if the state (1) made participation in a lynch mob a violation of state law and authorized its highest law enforcement officer to assume responsibility for prosecutions where a lynching occurred, and (2) authorized the trial to take place in a county other than the one in which the lynching took place, the United States Attorney General would not be authorized to seek indictments until it appeared after a reasonable time that the state was not seeking convictions in good faith. The two requirements were, of course, based upon the fact that often lynchers were not prosecuted because of a breakdown in the enforcement machinery as a result of race feeling and the local pressures that were applied to elected officials. A state officer was not subject to this pressure, at least not to the same degree. The requirement that the prosecution should be in another county was not emphasized. Perhaps this should have been taken out, but in an effort to make sure that exertions by the states were required, I included both of these qualifications.

4. *Fair Employment Practices Commission.* The FEPC had become the symbol of the civil rights cause and presented the greatest difficulties from the standpoint of sectional conflict. Still I did not believe it was beyond solution and was confident that we were much farther along than we were when the President first advanced his proposal for a federal compulsory statute. I studied this part of the report rather carefully and talked to many people who were familiar with the experience of the federal FEPC during the war period. That agency accomplished a good deal in behalf of minority groups, particularly Negro workers, who were being denied employment for which they were fitted. It was practically all accomplished, however, by counseling and not by coercive action, a good example being the Sun Oil Company case in Houston, where as a result of inducing the labor unions and management to accept a change of policy on Negro employment, the war effort was advanced and Negroes were admitted to types of employment to which they were entitled.

There could be no question about the magnitude of the problem or the fact that millions of Americans in minority groups, religious as well as racial, would continue to fight for policies in American industry that accorded all groups substantial equality. The question of compulsion loomed large in the controversy because of the belief by proponents that a federal statute without sanctions would result in little progress. Much of the FEPC debate also centered around the question of the respective jurisdictions of the state and federal governments. Many thoughtful students of the problem believed it would be a mistake for the federal government to force fair employment policies upon the states and that about the only kind of help federal authorities could give was to model an educational and voluntary program after the program for handicapped workers in an attempt to induce those who framed industrial policies, including organized labor unions, to adopt policies that would advance us toward the ideal of equality. To do more than this would cause deep cleavages between the races in Southern states and tend to cancel out any theoretical gains that might be made through a federal statute for the Negro people.

At the same time, I contended that if the Congress should set up a modest educational program we would acquire in time a body of experience that would be a guide to future legislation and would make available to all state officials the experience and results of legislation adopted by the states.

The above were the four main features of my plan, later referred to by the *San Francisco Chronicle* as "the Arkansas Plan," a phrase which I was glad to see used to help popularize the proposal. My program gradually won disciples throughout the nation and the South. Senator Russell of Georgia did not personally approve of all its features but told Mr. Truman that if it was accepted as a one-package compromise he would go along. Senator Russell's statement was probably the best boost my plan had. While I cannot claim that many members of Congress from Southern states approved of the proposal, a large number of my Southern colleagues, even those who would have voted against it, felt that it would be very much in the nation's interest to get a compromise adopted and the divisive agitation ended.

The *Atlanta Constitution* ran an article on the Arkansas Plan on February 7, 1949, applauding it as a "well-reasoned compromise program that should appeal to moderates on both sides of the question." The article closed by stating that "the Hays program is certainly worthy of careful consideration by all those who honestly would like to see some effective civil rights legislation enacted. It opens the way for a meeting of minds among the moderates, though the extremists may be expected to raise their voices in opposition on both sides."

As evidence that there was support for the Arkansas Plan from the liberal side, Lester Granger, Executive Director of the National Urban League, wrote to Mr. Truman that he was convinced that my proposal presented an intelligent compromise on a highly controversial subject. While he opposed the FEPC features of my plan, he enthusiastically endorsed my program for eliminating the poll tax by Constitutional amendment and for federal action after a lynching when the states fail to proceed. In the *New Amsterdam News*, he told his readers that "the compromise offered by Congressman Brooks Hays merits White House consideration." As he put it, "I honestly believe that a majority of our Negro voters would prefer to get something done about civil rights in *this* Congress—at the highest possible level—rather than maintain an absolutely intransigent position that produces nothing. If this involves readjustment of method, they will not accuse the White House of selling them down the river—not if the accomplished result provides an important part of our total demands." This was the philosophy of Uncle Nelson, "Half of something is better than all of nothing."

Since I have described in detail the one-package Arkansas Plan compromise, it might be in order to report on its fate. The Arkansas Plan was the victim of extremism on both sides, and none of the bills to implement its provisions ever came out of committee. Its value should be appraised, not in terms of tangible results but as a tremendous factor in clearing the atmosphere and making possible friendly discussion of a delicate and explosive issue.

With the abandonment of the compromise proposal, I began to weigh the merits of the individual measures, with these results:

(1) I have re-introduced at the opening of each session the equal employment opportunities bill (my version of FEPC). As previously indicated, this would authorize an educational and coordinating service by the Department of Labor in the field of employment opportunities for the minority group, following the pattern of provisions for women in industry. Since Congress was adamant and I believe will continue to be adamant in opposing coercive and punitive features in private employment, it seems apparent that a mistake was made by the proponents of legislation in this field in not seeking the type of action which my bill envisioned.

(2) The anti-lynching bill, which projected federal authority into the situation only where states failed to meet responsibilities for prosecutions where lynchings occur, has been re-introduced. This bill has the virtue of applying proper pressures on the states in recognizing the primary obligation of the states to prosecute offenders, and federal participation in prosecution is authorized under established criteria that will preserve this vital principle.

(3) The proposal for a Constitutional amendment to eliminate the poll tax as a prerequisite for voting was not re-introduced, and there were good reasons for abandonment of this idea when the package approach broke down. The poll-tax voting requirement had become a symbol of minority ambitions in the early days of civil rights controversy, and since there were some states imposing rigid and inflexible requirements designed historically to discourage minority participation, this was understandable. No such

condition exists today; changes in the economic condition of the Negro have altered the situation considerably, and since the five states which still retain the poll tax have all shown a preference for using this method of registering voters, there seemed to be no longer any reason for pressing for repeal of the poll tax.

The year 1950 was to see the bitter Congressional strife come to pass that I had tried desperately to avoid. Extremists in both Houses and from both sides were able to retard and restrain the efforts of moderates to provide significant advances in the rights of minority groups. The advice of such men as Senator Russell, on the one hand, and Mr. Granger, on the other, was ignored. According to the Washington *Evening Star* of July 13, 1950, over a year after my plan was offered for consideration, the biggest mistake was made by the Truman Administration when it rejected this proposal. The *Star* was confident that "many Southern members of Congress would have voted for the Hays plan as a simple way out of the deadlock on civil rights. With Administration backing, it would have gone through Congress."

Evidence of the difficulties created by the failure to accept my plan was the debate over the compulsory FEPC proposal offered by Representative Adam Clayton Powell of New York in the spring of 1949. This bill (H.R. 4453) would have created a national commission against discrimination in employment composed of seven members to be appointed by the President and confirmed by the Senate. Provision was also made for the creation on local, state, and regional levels of advisory conciliation councils to secure the maximum adoption by industry and labor of the fair employment practices prescribed by the act without invoking legal sanctions. Mr. Powell pointed out that "the experience of the states that have FEPC laws testifies that impressive results have been achieved through conciliation and mediation, and that rarely, if ever, are legal sanctions involved." He did prescribe enforcement powers for the national unit, however, calling on the Commission to investigate the sworn, written charges of persons claiming to be aggrieved, and, provided efforts at conciliation failed, he advocated that hearings be held in conformity with the Federal Administrative Procedure Act, issuing cease-and-desist orders in appropriate cases. It was just such proposed methods of enforcement that angered many members of Congress and caused the strength of the moderate position to deteriorate.

In the hope of achieving a better climate of opinion on this explosive issue, I chose to testify at the hearings of the special subcommittee of the Committee on Education and Labor which was chaired by Mr. Powell. I reiterated my opposition to discrimination and conceded that minority groups were adversely affected in certain respects by discriminatory practices. I made it clear that I was entirely sympathetic with the movement to secure for racial and religious minorities full rights under the Constitution. Here is how I put it:

Mr. Chairman, I know that emphasis is often given to things we oppose. I would prefer that emphasis be given to things I favor. It is inevitable in any issue as controversial as this that the negative attitude will receive the high lights, but I would much prefer that the committee remember the things I favor rather than the things I object to, and I should also like to add at that point that it has given me some pain to find myself in opposition to the efforts of a minority group—a racial group with whom I have worked in the South—in a matter that is of such importance to them. I have not enjoyed that position. I have spoken frankly and sincerely, but I have spoken with some sensibilities, and I feel, if I could make some contribution to the clearing of the atmosphere, that would be more important than any technical advice or counsel I might offer. I think it is more important at this stage that we all create an atmosphere in which the right solution might be sought than to come up with the perfectly correct answer to some of these specific questions.

While opposing the pending bills, I have in mind certain alternative proposals which I trust will receive consideration of the committee. It is my opinion that this committee has an opportunity to render a great public service by rejecting coercive measures which will result in aggravating the problem and to recommend, on the other hand, a constructive approach carefully defining that limited federal aspect of this general problem.

I did not oppose the use of federal services in counseling for non-discrimination and in pursuing educational methods in the Department of Labor or some other federal agency that might be invoked for the economic aid of Negroes and other groups without driving the employers to extremes of action.

Mr. Powell answered my plea by stating that "the chairmen of all the State [FEPC] Commissions who came before us all submitted statements emphasizing the need for enforcement power even though there was never recourse to it, but it wasn't that they didn't use it because it was unwise. They did not use it because it was not needed. The heart of this legislation must be conciliation. It must be in fact the heart of any legislation, and, in my humble opinion, must be conciliation rather than coercion." This position was not far removed from mine, but Mr. Powell insisted that the threat of force was essential to the success of the program. It was just this "waving the big stick" which would tend to create an explosive situation in the South. Despite our wide areas of general agreement, we could not reconcile this basic area of disagreement and we failed to interpret the same facts in the same way. Mr. Powell would not admit that this legislation would cause great unrest in those regions in which customs were being undermined. He refused to recognize any Constitutional consideration and denied that the restrictions on freedom of association were different from those imposed in other areas. I could only close this part of my testimony by commenting: "I want the advancement they [the Negroes] make to be a permanent gain and not a phony gain or a temporary gain, and I know as a reality, not dealing with the theory of it, that there are many situations in which the reaction of the white workers with whom they would be thrown would be such that it would be a disservice to him, and whatever the weekly wage, it would not be enough to offset the other damage."

When Congressman Burke of Ohio expressed his belief that it would be necessary to have a "switch in the closet or club in the corner" provision to back up the educational and cooperative work, I replied that soft pedalling the threat did not make it any less real. "We can speak of the fact that counseling will be the principal process, but if there is a penalty provision in the FEPC law, we have created a fear in the hearts of millions of people and it would be a tragic reversal of this trend toward justice, leading us to racial frictions rather than allaying them. No economic advantage to the minority group could ever offset the damage as a result of it and that is the reason I simply cannot understand why we should entertain for a moment a court provision in an effort to work toward a goal, which I admit is a desirable goal. I know we cannot afford to do that."

The "great debate" continued on into the next session of the Eighty-First Congress when I debated with Congressman Marcantonio the value of compulsory FEPC (H.R. 4453) as opposed to legislation I proposed to implement the Arkansas

Plan. I said then that "there never has been a time in recent years when the need for national unity is so great. While I differ profoundly with my friends who have urged this compulsory legislation upon the House, I recognize that there are some conditions throughout the country which explain the ferment of opinion which has brought the issue before us." I then tried to convince my colleagues that the Negro had made great progress, particularly during that past year, in equalizing educational and economic opportunities. In that regard, I continued:

There are those who offer the FEPC as a solution of one problem, who would agree that underlying that is a graver problem, a more fundamental problem, which is the education of our people. That does not have racial implications, except that of course for a long time, following their emergence from slavery, opportunities for the race were not abundant. Neither was the Negro always prepared to take advantage of such limited opportunities as were offered. It is no evidence at all of a lack of benevolence or humanitarian interest in the Negro on the part of the white majority that those opportunities were somewhat limited. I think it is a wholesome thing that the Negro has been insisting that opportunities be made more equal. Many measures for equalization awaited merely the insistence that they be granted. The interesting thing is that as the Negro asks for better opportunities in every field of endeavor he receives them. . . .

Now I am anxious not to misrepresent our Negro leaders; I am sure that the Negro leadership of the South theoretically stands opposed unanimously to compulsory segregation—they have said so. We recognize the implications of it, but the best proof in the world of their sound thinking is in the statement that a group of Negro leaders made in 1942, in the famous Durham Conference, that they recognized that the real progress to be made for their people must be within the framework of our own democracy in the Southern States; and I should add that no one should ask them to desist in their efforts to secure changes. But when it comes to a question of Federal policy, surely as practical men we should recognize that the decisions must be left to the States and to the localities....

Mr. Speaker, we are therefore dealing with a very fundamental problem—a problem that touches dangerous situations. It deals, too, with one of the foundation principles of our society which is that of a free industry. Whenever any law undertakes to say that an employer shall hire applicant A instead of applicant B and shall be fined or imprisoned for not following a Federal agency's decision as to which employees may be discharged, surely there are alerted dangers for us to consider. As reasonable men, as legislators with responsibilities to maintain a nonviolent community and a just order wherever Federal authority is projected, we are challenged to exhibit the finest intelligence and ingenuity that this House can summon....

Mr. Marcantonio rose to challenge my position. He claimed that my position of "gradualism" had been responsible for the fact that there had been no civil rights legislation since 1875. According to Mr. Marcantonio, "The gentleman has now just given us a marvelous picture of Jim Crow and segregation. I think the best answer to that question is the answer the Negro himself gives you. He refuses to live any longer under Jim Crow and segregation. He resents being treated as different from anybody else. So the gentleman may travel all over the world and try to make comparisons, and one may disagree as to comparisons, but that is not the point at all. The point is that we here in America have to face this problem. We have refused to face it since 1875." Here is a *Record* excerpt from my reply:

Mr. Hays of Arkansas. Not in my country have we refused to face it. We have worked pretty hard at it down in Arkansas. If I know the South, we have been working hard at it, and that is where 70 per cent of the American Negroes live. I agree, of course, that we should have as our standard—not the other countries' but the American ideal—an ideal still to be pursued for both races.

Mr. Marcantonio. If you have worked so hard at it, you have certainly cemented more than ever before your system of segregation and Jim Crow. That you cannot challenge. You know it is true. As a matter of fact, the gentleman's whole speech is based upon the perpetuation of that system.

Mr. Hays of Arkansas. I disagree with my friend from New York. I think the gentleman will look in vain for words of mine to sustain that statement.

Mr. Marcantonio. Will the gentleman yield further?

Mr. Hays of Arkansas. I yield.

Mr. Marcantonio. I thank the gentleman for yielding to me. I think the gentleman is eminently fair. I think he is doing a scholarly job here this afternoon and I, for one, appreciate the spirit in which he is conducting this discussion, although I disagree with him. The gentleman's position is, and I think if the gentleman reads back through his speech he will find it so, he has stated here that the system of segregation is one that exists, has existed, and must stand, and that we cannot change it. That is the gentleman's fundamental basis, is that not true?

Mr. Hays of Arkansas. I have said that changes to be made anywhere that there are harsh and cruel aspects of it must be made by the municipality or by the legislature and not by the Congress.

This exchange was not pitched on the emotional level that Mr. Marcantonio generally used in debate with members from the South. It was a most remarkable admission for him to make that anyone of the white race in Congress from south of the Mason-Dixon line could be "eminently fair." As the extremist champion of minority rights, he had built his reputation on fiery denunciation of those he considered the enemies of civil rights progress. The spectacle of Mr. Marcantonio of New York in reasoned debate with Mr. Hays of Arkansas astounded veteran reporters in the galleries.

Mr. Marcantonio viewed the proposed prohibition of discrimination in employment as the beginning of an attack on one phase of segregation. By refusing to accept an advisory FEPC as an educational device to promote fair treatment in the economic arena, he was forcing the Negro to judge all legislation by its contribution to breaking down the barriers of segregation rather than by its contributions to his general welfare as a citizen of the United States. While I had repeatedly commented on the aspects of segregation that I thought were not in accord with our professions of equality, it was my desire to aid the cause of all underprivileged minorities by creating a setting of better relations in the field of employment. As I saw it, any minority should realize that force bills are not in their interest. Certainly, the force bills following the Civil War were not in the Negro's interest. They retarded the progress of the Negro and caused a lot of bitterness and hardship. It was not a Southern Democrat who said that there was more bitterness caused following the Civil War by utterances in the halls of Congress than by incidents on the battlefields of the South.

I closed my presentation with a reminder to the Congress that

this idea of representative government is ours to cherish. I have justified my reference to my Negro constituents on that basis. I must not forget their interests. At the same time I have spoken with vigor on the question of force and with complete compatibility, I think, with this other sentiment because we will work against the Negro's interest if we adopt these measures of compulsion. The fact is that the interests of the races are bound together. . . .

It is a wise saying that the white man cannot hold the Negro in a ditch without staying there with him. . . .

The key to it all is justice. If there has been an element of suffering growing out of our poverty, something we do not speak of often and yet the complete picture requires it, the picture of eroded hills and limited markets, if we speak of suffering, it is because an element of suffering affects us all and draws us together. Emil Brunner put it like this, "All suffering is bitter. Suffering that is unjust is doubly bitter. Suffering that is of destiny unites. Suffering that is unjust divides."

We must heed the cry of suffering where it is said that it is the result of a faulty Federal policy. I want to meet that challenge, in order that there may be no suffering among any minority group, whether it is racial or religious, and in order that there should be no feeling that they are not wanted. Our Negro people, and every group, whatever their faith, are wanted in this great land.

It is up to us to work toward a policy of perfect justice for all men. And when our labors are done, I will be content if we apply that simple standard of justice for both worker and employer and find a greater unity in the happiness of people who resolve their conflicts on such a basis. It will fortify equal justice in the courts in the provision for equal facilities to all people in all public services and in equal opportunities for men of every race.

When the final debate on the Powell bill began on the floor of the House, Mr. McConnell proposed a substitute in which he attempted to remove the sanctions without changing the basic form of the proposal. This substitute, which was to pass the House by a significant margin, was unacceptable to me because it still had the form of force if not the complete substance. I was particularly concerned about a section which provided harsh penalties for interfering with the work of the proposed commission. Although Mr. McConnell's amendment proposed to eliminate the jail sentence and leave it on a fine basis, his bill still provided for investigatory powers and for the subpoena power. It also proceeded on the theory that cases would arise always because of a quarrel or dispute. I challenged this philosophy and objected to the fact that the bill created a "court" of five high-powered judges. They were to be called Commissioners, but they were, nevertheless, to operate under quasi-judicial procedures, choosing between two sides.

My bill proceeded on quite a different theory. As I pointed out in the debate,

by providing advisory councils, it emphasizes conciliation rather than coercion in the promotion of job opportunities. It establishes a fair employment practice agency in the Department of Labor and gives a mandate to carry out the philosophy of this bill. There is danger, therefore, if we adopt the theory of mediation rather than compulsion, in setting up a commission procedure to regard the parties as antagonists, as applicants for jobs that are not accepted, or as employees that are discharged, when actually the legislation is designed to advance us through educational methods towards a desirable goal. Now I think the House recognizes that I have come a long way to come to this point of conceding that some legislative action ought to be taken by the House on the problem. I think there are grave reasons why we should take action. . . . We ought to proceed consistently with this theory of mediation, leaving out all elements of compulsion.

When the bill passed the House containing these overtones of force, it was doomed to defeat in the Senate. It was the only bill of the more than seventy introduced in the period of the Seventy-Eighth through the Eighty-First Congresses, 1943-1950—my tenure in office till that time—to have succeeded in passing either House. In the Senate, extensive hearings were held in 1945, 1948, and 1949 on various FEPC proposals, and numerous reports were issued. S. 101 was the subject of a lengthy debate in 1946 and S. 1728 was the indirect subject of a nine-day-long debate in 1950 (the year the Powell bill passed the House). The numerous attempts to obtain a motion for the consideration of the proposals for such a program have failed, of course, because of Senate Rule 22 which sanctions unlimited debate (permitting filibusters). When the FEPC section of my Arkansas Plan was not accepted, all hope of Congressional action was lost.

CHAPTER FOUR

Politics and the Law

MY BACKGROUND IN THE CIVIL RIGHTS AREA NOW GAVE ME A greater voice in the deliberations of the Democratic party on the question of party policy towards minorities. I could speak with more assurance in view of the support my position had gained with Democrats from all parts of the country, and I looked forward to the opportunity of being of service at the 1952 Democratic Convention.

In 1951, even a year before the Convention, some members of Congress and others began to talk to me about the platform and the need of getting something like my Arkansas Plan through the Congress so that the Democratic party would have something to "point to with pride" instead of still "viewing with alarm" the failure to get civil rights proposals enacted into law. In the absence of some legislation it was feared that something as objectionable to the South as the 1948 declaration would absolutely be insisted upon and would be easy to get through the Democratic Convention, thus presenting another threat to party unity. All of this, of course, was looked at from the standpoint of party strategy, and the question of the merits of the controversial proposals was kept in the background. I think it was true of

some extremists of both sides that they preferred an issue
to a solution, but fortunately their number was small.

Two institutional loyalties had been unshaken throughout
my life—the Baptist church and the Democratic party. I
had often quoted the good brother who said in opposition
to the union of the Baptist and Christian churches, "I'm a
Baptist and nobody is going to make a Christian outa me!"
My devotion to the national Democratic party was almost
as firm. I was determined that nothing would make a Dixiecrat out of me, but I wanted the Democratic party to deserve
the sentimental attachment which so many of us in the South
continued to hold for it.

Although I continued to work on the legislative problem,
I got little encouragement from any of the party leaders.
Occasionally, people like Senator Mike Monroney would
say, "Keep at it. You have the answer." Senator Paul Douglas,
though committed to an all-out program, would sometimes
say something to encourage me. Hubert Humphrey, who
had just come to Washington like a whirlwind as the new
senator from Minnesota, after debating the issues with me
at George Washington University, mentioned my plan in a
complimentary way on the floor of the Senate. While he
remained as committed as ever to his strong principles on
the civil rights issue, he was willing to discuss any honest
approach to the subject. He could not permit any dilution
of the ends he hoped ultimately to achieve, but he was anxious to be as elastic as possible as to means. Occasionally,
also, Negro newspapermen, most notably Lester Granger,
would show up at my office to ask about some of the details
of my program, and they almost invariably evidenced appreciation for what I was trying to do. I had accepted an invitation to appear on a Town Hall Meeting of the Air to debate
race relations with Charles Johnson of Fisk University as
far back as April 18, 1950, and this early test of my proposals

turned out to get a very satisfactory reception. Most of my mail from the South was friendly, though two or three people berated me for not being more partisan and more violent in opposing Dr. Johnson's position. It was during this same period that Speaker Rayburn asked me to look over some civil rights bills sent to him for introduction. One of these bills provided for an FEPC which would have had far greater powers than the one called for in a compromise bill sponsored in the Senate by Senators Humphrey and Ives. The Humphrey–Ives proposal was to receive a great deal of attention before the Convention opened as a possible way out of the FEPC deadlock.

Hubert Humphrey and I got together at this time, and we had a talk about the possibilities of a compromise, both in the Congress and in the party platform. He was already convinced that the only chance of getting anything through on the poll tax and lynching, for example, lay in this direction. I discussed it with him at a luncheon, with just the two of us present, and when we got down to details we found the FEPC issue to be the only stumbling block to the kind of one-package (Arkansas Plan) agreement Senator Russell had expressed a willingness to accept. Senator Humphrey still thought that, instead of my voluntary non-sanctions agency in the Department of Labor, it would be necessary to set up in the Department of Justice a civil rights division with other interests than employment problems and with some more specific authority than my employment bureau would have.

We parted with the understanding that if we could work out something of the kind that would be eventually acceptable, we might undertake to promote it jointly, in such a way that it would appeal to our respective groups. We never got around to it. Late in 1951, in a newspaper interview, Hubert let go with a blast at all compromise efforts that seemed at the time to remove him from the circle of conciliation.

In the meantime, however, he had written a very good letter to Southern editors, and it had received some favorable notice in the South. In this 2,000-word letter to about twenty prominent Southern editors, he offered the region an olive branch, appealing for a "hearing" and "more understanding of our objectives."

He stated that civil rights was a national, and not just a local, issue and that a national party had to tell the American people where it stood on important national issues, however controversial. But he paid tribute to the Southern states for the progress many of them had achieved in enacting state laws against lynching, abolishing poll taxes, and for improvement in education, health, housing, and community facilities. He ended by stating his belief that both North and South were working for the same objectives: ". . . equal opportunity for all; the full rights of citizenship for all; full and equal protection of the law for all."

It was a significant document because, while Hubert made no specific concessions, he did seek to end the cleavage between the North and the South. Since he was the most prominent leader of the civil rights "champions" in 1948, his conciliatory attitude now gave us some hope of achieving accord in Chicago in 1952. We developed the kind of friendship that permits kidding without personal feeling. I told him after that letter that his actions reminded me of the man who said, "These divisions are just too bad—why can't we all just get together and everybody be Baptists."

I had just about despaired of getting anything done on my compromise plan until sometime in the spring of 1952 when John McCormack, House majority leader, rather casually told me that he and Speaker Rayburn had recommended me for membership on the preconvention Platform Drafting Committee. He told me very little about it; in fact, he identified no one else on the drafting committee at that time. After the personnel of the committee was announced, however, and it appeared that a harmonizing approach was clearly in the minds of Democratic party chairman, Frank McKinney, and other administration leaders, I concluded that the middle-of-the-road plan still had a chance.

Senator John Sparkman and I took the lead by organizing a breakfast meeting. As I recall it, not a single person invited to that breakfast failed to attend. I asked John McCormack if he wanted to be invited, but he thought perhaps Congressman Mike Kirwan and I might represent the House, and, to make it clear that the meeting was not tied in officially with the Convention platform plans, he decided not to come, since he was scheduled to be chairman of the full Platform Committee. Present at the meeting were the following: Kirwan and I from the House; Sparkman, Fulbright, Monroney, Magnuson, Lehman, Green, Humphrey, and Douglas from the Senate. The discussion was thorough and frank on the part of everyone. Hubert Humphrey had learned more about the details than any of the others on his side and felt that something might be done to satisfy both sides. Governor Lehman was our biggest problem. He was sure that nothing less than a compulsory FEPC would be accepted and served notice that he would fight for that kind of party declaration. On other phases of the program he was just as unyielding, still he thought we should try hard to avoid a split.

Mike Monroney's suggestion—and it was echoed by others —that Humphrey and I sit down together to work out suitable language produced a rather interesting retort from the Senator. Hubert said, "I will not let my persuasive friend from the South—much as I like him—I will not let Brooks Hays dilute my conviction on civil rights. I will not get into any kind of conference or any kind of drafting committee that will embarrass me in case I decide to go before that convention to plead for an all-out 100 per cent declaration on civil rights." He said a lot more, but that was the substance of it. Still, his cordial feeling toward me was intact and when I left him I got a smile out of him by saying, "Hubert, you are a prophet of righteousness and you know I respect your sincerity. You belong in the Old Testament. You might remember, though that even the Old Testament prophets were able to speak with a prophetic voice because they knew how sinners thought and acted, and maybe you ought to know a little more about how we who are less than 100 per cent from your point of view on civil rights feel about some of these problems." Much of the credit for whatever success we had at this meeting was due to John Sparkman, who proved to be a good influence on all of us.

A couple of months before the Convention was held, Governor Paul Dever of Massachusetts, already chosen to be keynoter, made a statement on nation-wide television that reflected a spirit of compromise among party strategists. He observed that personally he saw little difference between the 1948 plank and the more moderate one of 1944, and he indicated his belief that the 1944 version would be satisfactory this year. He expected "neither side to surrender completely" and agreed that "there must be concessions by both sides," but he declared himself "hopeful the Platform Committee will draft a plank on civil rights which will be universally acceptable."

The Dever speech brought forth a roar of protest from the liberal wing of the party. Francis Biddle spoke for the ADA when he answered Dever by predicting that the "little difference will spell victory or defeat for the Democratic Party in 1952."

"The question confronting the country today," Mr. Biddle

wrote to Mr. Dever, "is not whether the Democratic Party can effect a strategic retreat or even stand the ground it has gained during the two New Deal–Fair Deal decades. The important question is whether it has the courage and vigor to move forward. In our opinion one of the most important advances it must make is to spell out even more clearly the implications of the 1948 civil rights plank by calling for a revised Senate rule to end filibusters."

Walter Reuther provided a plan for achieving this goal, designed to break the grip of the South on all civil rights legislation. As he saw it, "The try must be made the moment after the new Senate is convened and new members are sworn. The try can and will succeed—if the Vice-President and a majority of the Senators then in the floor are prepared to stand up and be counted in support of this single proposition; that the Eighty-Third Senate is a new Senate, with the same full power under the Constitution to write its own rules that were enjoyed and exercised by the First Senate." Thus Rule 22, which requires a two-thirds vote to stop filibusters, would be discarded. Any such move to permit majority vote to govern Senate debate would obviously outrage the South, and giving it platform support would certainly split the Democratic party again.

Speaking of filibusters and the growth of public interest in the pros and cons regarding their continuance, I was reminded of the new increased usage of the term in common conversation one morning as I was about to get on a train in Washington's Union Station. I saw a young Negro woman urging a small boy toward the train, but the youngster was dragging his feet very effectively and indulging in a fit of temper. His mother reassured him but was plainly fast losing her patience. I was wondering whether I should try to help her when a Negro soldier came along and sized up the situation. With hardly a pause in his stride, he picked up the recalcitrant boy, mounted the train steps, and deposited him in a vacant seat, saying firmly:

"Now you listen to me, you think about yo' mama. You quit filibusterin'!"

With regard to the FEPC issue, the talk of compromise continued. My Arkansas Plan proposal was often referred to, and the bill I mentioned earlier, introduced jointly by Senators Humphrey and Ives, became the focal point of preconvention discussion. The bill had been approved by the Senate Committee on Labor and Public Welfare shortly before the Eighty-Second Congress had adjourned. Northern members of the Platform Committee of a moderate bent were striving for a civil rights plank that, while it might not please the South, would not incite revolt. It was recalled that in Congress, where legislation such as the Humphrey–Ives bill must clear committees, Southern Democrats were in control and should not be antagonized. The hope was that some way could be found to encourage all forty-eight states to set up FEPC's, without arousing the ire of the Southern senators.

The compromise proposal contained provisions which were designed just for the purpose of encouraging the individual states to handle their own civil rights problems. Emphasis was placed, however, on the fact that where the states did not handle this problem, the federal government would step in. This federal FEPC would have the authority to issue subpoenas to witnesses, hold hearings, and also make recommendations for the settlement of complaints—but without resorting to the issuance of cease-and-desist orders to enforce its recommendations for a period of at least one year; at the end of the waiting period, the federal law would become binding on all states which had failed to adopt FEPC's of their own.

The compromise factor of the federal government's keeping hands off in states that had their own anti-discrimination

laws was the creation of Northern liberals who hoped
to gain Southern acceptance. Their olive branch was not
likely to be accepted because, unlike my proposal, the
federal commission would have the power to try alleged
violations of the anti-discrimination law and Southern states
would not be permitted to write laws that had no enforcement clauses. One indication that there might be trouble
ahead was the comment of Adlai Stevenson, at that time
Governor of Illinois, who was known as a moderate on civil
rights and who was under consideration for the nomination
for president: "In Illinois, I have tried earnestly to effect
the adoption of a fair employment practices law with power
of enforcement. I feel very strongly this is the first responsibility of the states themselves. If the states are unwilling or
unable (to prevent job discrimination), then I presume there
is no alternative to having the federal government do so."

To make matters worse, Northern liberals of the ADA
school were against any moderation on the FEPC issue. The
industrial Northeast was the center of activities of liberal,
labor, and minority groups, and the representatives of this
region believed it would be fatal to the Democratic party
to "give one inch" on such a symbolic matter as FEPC.
When Averell Harriman entered the presidential primaries
and produced a stunning upset over Estes Kefauver in the
District of Columbia, this was pointed to as proof of the
strength of a strong civil rights stand, since Harriman made
FEPC the central theme of his addresses, while Kefauver
counseled moderation. So I arrived in Chicago in advance
of the Convention which began on July 21, 1952, with less
than full confidence in the success of my mission.

John Sparkman and I got together early and often in
Chicago, and I benefited greatly from our conversations on
the civil rights issue. We were both anxious to keep our
Southern colleagues informed of our activities, and Senator

Russell of Georgia for one seemed pleased with the compromise approach we were making. Before we concluded our preliminary discussions, we knew fairly well what our strategy would be. One thing I think was especially important: we agreed that during the public hearings, when Walter White of the NAACP and others would vigorously present the civil rights position, we would remain silent and take whatever they wanted to throw at us. Actually Mr. White was not very caustic himself, though some of the spokesmen for his group were bitter toward the South, even toward Senator Sparkman. We lived up to our resolution; we did not complain or fight back. I think it helped considerably.

It is important to note that Hubert Humphrey was not a member of the Platform Committee during this convention, an omission which certainly must have created some unhappiness among the liberals. Senator Lehman took over their mantle of leadership and continued to exhibit militant feelings about the civil rights proposals. At times his attitude led me to be rather discouraged about getting something accomplished in the Committee. Labor union leaders were among his supporters and told the platform writers that if they stood for "people against privileges," the party would be continued in power. The Harriman bloc appeared eager for an FEPC showdown, hinting at an ultimatum that they get a "maximum" plank in the Committee or else they would force a floor fight. As they put it, they "would settle for nothing less than 100 per cent of the Roosevelt and Truman programs." Also Senator Benton of Connecticut said: "A strong civil rights plank was so important to the survival of the American people" that an all-out fight for one would be worth the risk of another Southern bolt.

This attitude made me quite apprehensive about the Northern liberals' carrying out their threat of a floor fight, even if the moderates should win by the vote of the full Platform Committee. A repeat of the 1948 experience would then be likely. It was at that time that John Sparkman and I decided that Hubert Humphrey might be persuaded to help us prevent a split. We asked him to have breakfast with us in John's room at the Congress Hotel. This was a crucial stage in the proceedings, after the public hearings had been completed and the actual drafting in the subcommittee was getting underway. We let Hubert understand, as we had given all others to understand, that on some points we would be just as unyielding as he. We were willing to go pretty far. We would personally take responsibility for language committing the party to a civil rights program with appropriate federal action, and we would go home to defend that kind of party commitment, but we could not defend the use of the words "compulsory FEPC" or any other phrase such as "enforceable" that would project federal authority into the situation.

A point that I had difficulty making stick with both sides was that a compromise could not be justified that did not rest upon logic. The moderate should not ask for compromises down "the middle of the road" just to get peace in the family. I used this illustration: If one argued, for example, that two plus two equals six and attempted to compromise with one who held to the answer four, he would hardly get anywhere by suggesting that they split the difference and make it five. If the Northern liberals held to the idea of a federal coercion in matters of private employment, I saw no basis for compromise.

On the question of the Senate rules, we also worried that the advocacy of repeal of Rule 22 or the use of such words as "cloture" or "filibuster" would have the same effect as the Convention action in 1948. Senator Lehman appeared likely to carry this appeal to the Convention, since he was championing a rules change by which two-thirds of the senators could halt debate after two days, but only a simple majority would be needed after fifteen days.

We stepped up our efforts to explore the possibilities of a compromise. While Hubert had not changed his fundamental position, he did assure us that he would not make a floor fight, and he expressed the hope that we would get something that everyone could live with. It remained to be seen how much his conciliatory attitude would help us achieve unity.

Platform Chairman John McCormack was doing his utmost to prevent a split without cutting the heart out of the Northern position. He had been convinced all along that John Sparkman and I were right in standing for party harmony. He was with us on that, even though he stood for strong federal civil rights legislation. His conciliatory spirit would undoubtedly raise problems for him in the North, and we were just as anxious as he was that he hold the confidence of the other side. We had few conferences with him —just an occasional word or two, and nothing dealing with language. Since all the newspapermen knew that John Sparkman and I were working on this crucial problem, however, we were carrying quite a burden from the standpoint of the South. Much of our efforts were designed to mollify such men as Platform Committee member B. D. Murphy, a lawyer from Atlanta. His views were reasonably close to those of Senator Russell, although philosophically he was much farther to the Right and was willing to compromise only for the purpose of helping Russell and holding the party together.

As the platform writers were proceeding gingerly on this sensitive civil rights language, a new complication arose. Convention outbreaks over the loyalty pledge were finally resolved by an agreement to require each delegate merely to use every honorable means of getting the Democratic party's candidates on his state ticket without forcing him to violate any law of his state. The bitterness engendered by this clash required even more delicate negotiations than before. Word was received from the more conservative Southern ranks that the civil rights plank would now "have to be entirely innocuous" in order to get through without serious intraparty repercussions. John Sparkman tried to allay such fears by announcing that he saw a good chance for the civil rights plank to be accepted by the Convention without serious, if any, floor fighting.

I was constantly in touch with John Sparkman during this time, but I was not on the final drafting committee. I was scheduled to be on that subcommittee, but John McCormack told me that, because I was not a delegate, he feared that my appointment would weaken our case, since my status undoubtedly would be challenged. This was a keen disappointment to John Sparkman and he argued mildly with John McCormack about it, but I think the chairman was right. The only result of this decision was some inconvenience for John Sparkman in keeping me informed of what was going on in working out suitable language for the draft. From time to time, I would see John, and I even went into the subcommittee room one time to get information. While every non-member was theoretically excluded from that committee, I think no one objected to my having this contact with Sparkman.

The main civil rights section was finally agreed upon by both the drafting committee and the final Platform Committee. John Sparkman and I were victors in the showdown vote! This success was achieved because of a willingness to include two other sections in the platform, one on Constitutional government and the other on improving Congressional procedures, these sections providing diplomatic lan-

guage on matters in which advocacy was demanded by each
extreme. More about these sections further on, but first let
us look at the civil rights section. It reads as follows:

The Democratic Party is committed to support and advance the
individual rights and liberties of all Americans.

Our country is founded on the proposition that all men are
created equal. This means that all citizens are equal before the
law and should enjoy equal political rights. They would have
equal opportunities for education, for economic advancement, and
for decent living conditions.

We will continue our efforts to eradicate discrimination based
on race, religion, or national origin.

We know this task requires action, not just in one section of
the Nation, but in all sections. It requires the cooperative efforts
of individual citizens and action by State and local governments.
It also requires Federal action. The Federal Government must
live up to the ideals of the Declaration of Independence and must
exercise the powers vested in it by the Constitution.

We are proud of the progress that has been made in securing
equality of treatment and opportunity in the Nation's Armed
Forces and the civil service and all areas under Federal jurisdiction. The Department of Justice has taken an important part in
successfully arguing in the courts for the elimination of many
illegal discriminations, including those involving rights to own
and use real property, to engage in gainful occupations, and to
enroll in publicly supported higher educational institutions. We
are determined that the Federal Government shall continue such
policies.

At the same time we favor Federal legislation effectively to
secure these rights to everyone: (1) the right to equal opportunity for employment; (2) the right to security of persons;
(3) the right to full and equal participation in the Nation's political life, free from arbitrary restraints. We also favor legislation
to perfect existing Federal civil rights statutes and to strengthen
the administrative machinery for the protection of civil rights.

The platform group did not mention FEPC by name in its statement, but it did include much of what had been quite controversial in 1948. The civil rights plank fell short of demands made by President Truman, but neither he nor Franklin Roosevelt had been able to get such programs through Congress for two decades. Instead of a plank pledging "enforceable" federal laws, the final draft advocated "federal legislation effectively to secure these rights." A resolution of this conflict had been arrived at under the pressure of North–South bargaining.

In accordance with our agreement, we managed to work out an acceptable statement related to Constitutional principles. Its purpose was to commit the party to recognize Constitutional limitations in carrying out the platform mandates. We had discussed adding to the civil rights statement a phrase to the same effect, but gave it up in favor of a more comprehensive reference to our belief in a proper balance between federal and state authority. I was assigned the job of preparing the statement and wrote it at six o'clock one morning in the Palmer House. The Committee accepted my language and put it into the platform as follows:

The Democratic Party has demonstrated its belief in the Constitution as a charter of individual freedom and an effective instrument for human progress. Democratic administrations have placed upon the statute books during the last 20 years a multitude of measures which testify to our belief in the Jeffersonian principle of local control, even in general legislation involving Nation-wide programs. Selective service, social security, agricultural adjustment, low-rent housing, hospital, and many other legislative programs have placed major responsibilities in States and counties and provide fine examples of how benefits can be extended through Federal-State cooperation.

In the present world crisis with new requirements of Federal action for national security, and accompanying provision for public services and individual rights related to defense, constitutional principles must and will be closely followed. Our record and our clear commitments in this platform measure our strong faith in the ability of constitutional government to meet the needs of our times.

Turning to the problem of Rule 22 and the filibuster, the Platform Committee agreed to include a section advocating improvement of Congressional procedures. This plank had been insisted upon by President Truman, whose suggestion of language to the Platform Committee, however, was open to several interpretations. Thus the Committee was able to write a general statement of basic principles: "In order that the will of the American people may be expressed upon all legislative proposals, we urge that action be taken at the beginning of the Eighty-third Congress to improve Congressional procedures so that majority rule prevails and decisions can be made after reasonable debate without being blocked by a minority in either House."

While Mr. Truman and other liberals had wanted a stronger attack on the filibuster and a definite commitment on the part of senators and senatorial candidates to do their best from the start of the new Congress in January to change the Senate rule permitting filibusters, the platform did go along in a general way and even included the Rules Committee of the House in its recommendation. It is true that "majority rule" was left undefined, but the President's message itself had not made clear whether he meant majority of those voting or majority of the total Senate or House membership. This plank was definitely a victory for the liberal forces on the Committee. While John Sparkman and I, like many Southerners, took the position that any change in Rule 22 of the Senate or any procedures of the House Rules Committee were matters for the Congress to decide and should not be considered in the Democratic platform, we yielded on this point in order to get the moderate platform adopted.

When the platform was brought before the Convention delegates, it was approved by a voice vote! This quick approval was aided immeasurably by the skillful parliamentary direction of Chairman Sam Rayburn, but it did represent widespread North–South acceptance, if not all-out support of the compromise proposals.

The unhesitating gavel and parliamentary precision Mr. Rayburn used did not impair his reputation for extreme fairness. He used haste only where delays and uncertainty in the chair would have invited extended argument and plunged the assembly into dissension. Any delegate requesting in advance an opportunity to protest some action was always given recognition.

The great majority of delegates of both sides were anxious to reduce the threat of continuing intraparty battles and reacted accordingly. Despite their deep concern for the many other grave problems of the country, the civil rights issue commanded their major attention. This was obvious when, just before midnight on Wednesday, John McCormack began to read the platform's final draft to the Convention —uppermost in the minds of all the delegates was "civil rights." It was with great pride that I watched them adopt the fruits of the labors of so many dedicated men.

While Senator Lehman never gave up and had to be defeated by both the committees, he did not carry the fight to the Convention floor. What all the influences were that kept him from this action I do not know, but the conciliatory attitude of Hubert Humphrey may well have been a significant factor. John McCormack's strategy was also very effective in the committees: he put the issue to a vote only when he was certain what the result would be and he handled Senator Lehman skillfully and always with kind-

ness. In the last analysis, of course, the 1952 platform statement, while moderate and less provocative to the South
than the 1948 one, would never have been accepted by the
South in 1948. This knowledge undoubtedly gave the liberals
enough satisfaction to hold them quiet.

With regard to the reaction of the South, when spokesmen
of the South arose to protest, Mr. Rayburn announced that
their protest came too late. He ruled that he had already
gaveled the instrument through to formal acceptance. Governor Herman Talmadge of Georgia sprang up, shouting that
his delegation demanded to be put on the record as voting
"No." Meanwhile, a similar demand came in the form of a
note to the chair from Governor Hugh White of Mississippi.
Mr. Rayburn let those entries go into the record but continued to hold that the platform had been adopted before
the protests were entered. One evidence that the platform
was generally acceptable to many delegates from the deep
South was the fact that Senator Russell allowed his name
to go before the Convention as a presidential candidate *after*
the platform had been adopted.

In looking back over the procedural development of the
1952 platform, I cannot say enough in tribute to McCormack
and Sparkman for the work they did in pulling us through
the Chicago Convention. I think it is fair to say that this
platform also represented a victory for the moderate point of
view with which I have been identified. This represented a
gain for those of us who wanted to hold the party together,
but involved something more than that. It recognized that
there was a job to be done and that the constructive phases
of the civil rights program should have recognition. In other
words, neither side can be said to have had its way. Those
who inclined to Mr. Truman's all-out program did not win
in Chicago. If they had had their way, the phrase "compulsory FEPC" and other expressions which constitute rally-

ing cries for minority groups would have gotten into the platform language. It is even futile to argue that the 1952 platform was stronger than 1948; the background was so different that any attempt to relate the actions of the two conventions would prove fruitless. Specifically, it was the reference to President Truman's civil rights message that provoked the walkout in 1948. Otherwise the commitments in 1952 were about as broad as in the 1948 Philadelphia Convention. From my standpoint, however, it is important to point out that the efforts to include such words as "compulsory," "enforceable," and "sanctions" were all defeated. The word "effective" did appear in the 1952 platform and that was acceptable to those of us who believed that extreme action was not only improper under our Constitution but would be ineffective.

During the 1952 presidential campaign, it became apparent that both General Eisenhower and Governor Stevenson were proposing action almost identical with a part of my 1949 Arkansas Plan, namely, that it was primarily the duty of the states to provide fair employment policies and to establish, through appropriate action, equality of opportunity in employment. Governor Stevenson read with approval the section on Constitutional government which I wrote for the Democratic platform in his speech in Nashville, Tennessee. While Stevenson was also supporting action by the federal government of a coercive sort to augment state action on FEPC, he was primarily concerned with the establishment of a federal policy aimed at realizing the legitimate aspirations of minority groups. It was just such a policy that the 1952 Democratic platform set forth for the American people.

What Adlai Stevenson would have done to carry out the Democratic platform will never be known, but the Republican victory was not followed by positive legislative action of any kind in the civil rights area. Actually, the whole focus of interest was changing from Congress to the judiciary, as the NAACP began to push through the lower courts the series of cases that directly challenged all segregation in public schools. It was obvious that the Supreme Court would soon have to face one of the gravest issues of the century. My own concern was very great. When Virginius Dabney asked my opinion for an article he was preparing for *The Saturday Evening Post* (published on November 8, 1952), I told him, "Any act of Congress or any order of the Supreme Court abolishing segregation and overriding the states in this vital matter would not only damage race relations but would also tend to cancel out the tremendous and steady gains being made by our Negro citizens."

Before the Supreme Court handed down its first decision —in fact, less than a week before, on May 12, 1954—I did take a stand against segregation in the important area of interstate transportation. I testified before the Committee on Interstate and Foreign Commerce on the proposal introduced by Mr. Heselton of Massachusetts (H.R. 7304) designed to end the patchwork pattern of handling the seating or accommodations for passengers traveling in interstate commerce. Still fixed in my memory was that train ride I had taken as a boy when the Negro passengers had been crowded into the rear of the car while there were still many vacant seats in the white section. I had often wondered what the effect would have been of removing the rope dividing the sections or at least moving it forward so that all passengers could ride in comfort. I told the Committee that the Supreme Court decisions in this field made non-segregation in interstate transportation of passengers our national policy and left little to be done by federal authority. Because of the confusion that this decision had caused, I agreed that "it is wise for the Congress to make clear the fact that there is a policy of the national community and that interstate travel must be governed by that policy of non-segregation."

I then emphasized my belief that the Supreme Court decisions constituted the right policy. "The reason it is right policy, regardless of one's view as to *intra*state travel, is that passengers moving from St. Louis, Missouri, to Little Rock, Arkansas, for example, all pay the same fare, but if at the state line one is required to move into another coach, he has not had equal protection under the law."

My concern with the international aspects of this problem led me to comment, "As a member of the Foreign Affairs Committee, I have gradually swung around to the view that foreign policy is affected. Consider, for example, the colored passenger from another country. I am eager for him to carry back good impressions although I know the Communists are not going to let any efforts of ours toward justice be fairly presented to the world. I am not suggesting that we make our decisions on the basis of global strategy in this vital struggle with communism. It is a question of right dealing rather than strategy. But I want those who visit us to have when they go back home the most effective arguments it is possible for them to have when they talk in behalf of our country. I know in interstate travel we can do it."

While I could not support a bill which made federal decisions in areas which should be left to the states, I recognized that the federal aspects of this legislation did not do violence to the powers of the states. It was my desire to remove this proposal from the arena of bitter partisan politics. After making this clear, I said: "I think that we cannot in situations like this, though, escape the fact we do fill two roles— we are both moralist and lawmaker. Sometimes it is important to let the moralist carry some causes and not the lawmaker, and that underlies some of the things I have said. There have been many times when I wanted to agree with someone who differed with me on this conservative approach. I wanted to agree with him substantively, but as a lawmaker I could not consistently do so because, first, this is a dual form of government with some powers reserved to the States, and second, unless the sentiment of the people sustains a certain move, no matter how abstractly noble that objective is, then frustation will follow."

In order to avoid the possibility of any minority group's promoting its legitimate aims by encouraging "political" prosecution, I suggested the following amendment to the Heselton bill: "Where an act which constitutes a misdemeanor is committed in a State, and constitutes a criminal offense under a law of such State, no Federal court shall have jurisdiction of the offense against section 2 [of the Heselton bill] unless the court finds that the prosecution of the offense against State law has been impaired by the willful failure or refusal of a State law enforcement officer to perform his duties with respect to such prosecution."

Mr. Springer, one of the Committee members, raised the valid point that we would run into questions of proof as to whether or not the state had acted or had willfully failed to act. My feeling was that this question could be left to the sound discretion of the federal courts in which federal jurisdiction was claimed. As I saw it, the federal court should be required to find affirmatively that the state had not acted.

In summary, here is how my amendment would work in practice. If the Justice Department believed that at a particular place there was segregation of passengers traveling in interstate commerce, federal attorneys could bring suit against the responsible company officials in the local federal district court. The federal judge could then refuse to accept jurisdiction of the case if he found that there was a state law in effect barring such segregation and that the state law-enforcement officers were not willfully failing to make prosecutions under that state law. One Southern member of the Commerce Committee protested that "we would be handing the Attorney General quite a dangerous club to hold over the States," to compel them to make and enforce anti-segregation laws of their own. But I took a broader view: "I think that if the club idea were to cause us to refrain ultimately from getting into this kind of lawmaking, we would cut ourselves off from some good legal practices. There may be certain other areas besides civil rights in which there need to be directives to the Attorney General not to indulge in 'political' prosecution."

My support of this anti-segregation bill for travel in interstate commerce was ultimately based on the need to uphold the Constitution of the United States. I regarded the action of this bill by the Congress as a kind of test for the future. I said at that time: "I think you may find in this piece of legislation an opportunity to evaluate these sharp conflicts, and that you may rather welcome this as a chance to demonstrate what good legal minds can do with a problem that involves different social backgrounds, and you may bring into focus the interesting and variegated social communities that make up this nation." I expressed my optimism concerning the outcome and even registered "a mild dissent from the statement that a lot of people fear this sort of thing. I might point out I have talked only about transportation and I have not suggested a Federal statute with reference to segregation policies outside of transportation, and generally with reference to interstate travel. My opinion is that there would not be many islands of resistance to this general policy." I used this analogy to deal with the painful aspects of ending segregation in interstate travel: "It is like a corn on your toe. There may be other ailments more serious that require the doctor's treatment, but the corn is going to continue to cry out until you do something about it." One of my colleagues from Arkansas offered the rejoinder: "But at the same time, we are trying to do something about this corn, we do not want to develop a bunion, which hurts worse." I agreed with this note of caution, but felt that the end of segregation in interstate transportation would heal the corn without dangerous complications.

It gave me great pleasure to remind the members of the Committee of the progress that Arkansas had made. It had been only a dozen years previously that another member of the House of Representatives, a Negro, the Honorable Arthur Mitchell, had been taken off a Pullman in my state in the middle of the night. Mr. Mitchell brought suit to invalidate the Arkansas segregation policy on interstate trains, and his success in the Supreme Court was one of the groundbreaking decisions in this field. Other Negroes could now seek to expand this principle by private suit, but I spoke for this proposed legislation to enable the government to assume the burden and expense of prosecuting cases. It made me "right proud" to report that "in Arkansas itself, the policy of the Mitchell decision was accepted because of the Court's support," and such an episode as Mr. Mitchell's humiliation "was not likely to happen today, partly because train officials and fellow passengers think and act differently. ... In Arkansas the common practice is to accept non-segregation generally on trains that move interstate, as most of them do."

The Supreme Court decision of May 17, 1954, is too well known to need extensive quotation. The Court swept aside completely the doctrine of "separate but equal" schools for Negro children, first enunciated in the *Plessy v. Ferguson* decision of 1896, with the words, "We conclude that in the field of public education the doctrine of 'separate but equal' has no place. Separate educational facilities are inherently unequal." Less well known, except for the phrase "with all deliberate speed," are the provisions to implement the Supreme Court's decision spelled out the following year. We shall probably have to cope with these directives for many years, and it is worthwhile quoting them at some length.

Full implementation of these constitutional principles may require solution of varied local school problems. School authorities have the primary responsibility for elucidating, assessing, and solving these problems; courts will have to consider whether the action of school authorities constitutes good faith implementation of the governing constitutional principles. Because of their proximity to local conditions and the possible need for further hearings, the courts which originally heard these cases can best perform this judicial appraisal. Accordingly, we believe it appropriate to remand the cases to those courts.

In fashioning and effectuating the decrees, the courts will be guided by equitable principles. Traditionally, equity has been characterized by a practical flexibility in shaping its remedies and by a facility for adjusting and reconciling public and private needs. These cases call for the exercise of these traditional attributes of equity power. At stake is the personal interest of the plaintiffs in admission to public schools as soon as practicable on a nondiscriminatory basis. To effectuate this interest may call for elimination of a variety of obstacles in making the transition to school systems operated in accordance with the constitutional principles set forth in our May 17, 1954, decision. Courts of equity may properly take into account the public interest in the elimination of such obstacles in a systematic and effective manner. But it should go without saying that the vitality of these constitutional principles cannot be allowed to yield simply because of disagreement with them.

While giving weight to these public and private considerations, the courts will require that the defendants make a prompt and reasonable start toward full compliance with our May 17, 1954, ruling. Once such a start has been made, the courts may find that additional time is necessary to carry out the ruling in an effective manner. The burden rests upon the defendants to establish that such time is necessary in the public interest and is consistent with good faith compliance at the earliest practicable date. To that end, the courts may consider problems related to administration, rising from the physical condition of the school plant, the school transportation system, personnel, revision of school districts and attendance areas into compact units to achieve a system of determining admission to the public schools on a nonracial basis, and revision of local laws and regulations which may be necessary in solving the foregoing problems. They will also consider the adequacy of any plans the defendants may propose to meet these problems and to effectuate a transition to a racially nondiscriminatory school system. During this period of transition, the courts will retain jurisdiction of these cases.

The calm that initially prevailed in the South was eventually broken by the establishment of White Citizens Councils and the increased activity of the NAACP. These two groups met head on in the attempt by Miss Autherine Lucy to gain admission to the University of Alabama. In the Congress of the United States the turmoil was reflected in the debate over the bill to provide federal aid to education by means of grants for school construction. Congressman Adam Clayton Powell of New York introduced an amendment to deny funds to any school district that operated segregated schools. It was in this setting that the great majority of Southern congressmen and senators came together to issue the now-famous Declaration of Constitutional Principles or the so-called "Southern Manifesto." The declaration stated the views of over 100 members of the delegations of eleven Southern states as follows:

We regard the decision of the Supreme Court in the school cases as a clear abuse of judicial power. It climaxes a trend in the Federal Judiciary undertaking to legislate, in derogation of the authority of Congress, and to encroach upon the reserved rights of the States and the people. . . .

In the case of *Plessy v. Ferguson* in 1896, the Supreme Court expressly declared that under the Fourteenth Amendment no person was denied any of his rights if the States provided separate but equal public facilities. This decision has been followed in many other cases. It is notable that the Supreme Court, speaking through Chief Justice Taft, a former President of the United States, unanimously declared in 1927 in *Lum v. Rice* that the "separate but equal principle is . . . within the discretion of the State in regulating its public schools and does not conflict with the Fourteenth Amendment."

This interpretation, restated time and again, became a part of the life of the people of many of the States and confirmed their habits, customs, traditions, and way of life. It is founded on elemental humanity and common sense, for parents should not be deprived by government of the right to direct the lives and education of their own children. . . .

We pledge ourselves to use all lawful means to bring about a reversal of this decision which is contrary to the Constitution and to prevent the use of force in its implementation.

I signed this declaration as a proper statement of the South's objections to the overthrow of the *Plessy v. Ferguson* decision and violation of the *stare decisis* principle in Constitutional law. While it contained items which to me would have been better omitted and expressed some sentiments in language not to my liking, I believed the declaration was an honest reaction to the injury the South believed had been done to its way of life. I joined with a number of other members of Congress who refused to sign the document unless it removed all mention of the doctrines of nullification and interposition. In this way, the Southern moderates hoped to preserve the Constitutional guarantee of the right to dissent without advocating measures which might do violence to the Constitution.

The Court's interpretation reminded me that Senator Samuel Ervin, who was a justice of the North Carolina Supreme Court before becoming senator, once related an incident which might well be pondered by members of the judiciary. Senator Ervin chided an associate on the state Supreme Court by putting a sign on his door, following a liberal construction of a will (to which Ervin dissented), "Wills rewritten here." The following week, after Ervin himself had voted for a liberal construction of a statute, he found a sign on his own door reading, "General Assembly in Session."

As the tensions in the South increased, men of good will everywhere grew concerned about the breakdown of the good race relations which had been painstakingly developed in this area. During the same period that the "Manifesto" was issued, the spring of 1956, Erwin D. Canham, Editor of the *Christian Science Monitor*, requested a few elected officials and educators from Southern states to present constructive suggestions as to ways of preserving the basic areas of understanding and tolerance. Here is the telegram I sent in response to his request:

Situation in parts of South extremely serious but strains on interracial harmony can be relieved by exertions of both races. I commend you for previous efforts to interpret Southern viewpoints to the nation and your current effort to prevent further deterioration. Most of the aims of minority group were being steadily realized prior to Supreme Court decisions. Good faith efforts to live by rule-of-law tradition have been interrupted by extremists on both sides.

South properly resents every form of threat to enforce immediate and complete integration by Federal power, and difficulties are compounded by such threats. Protests and reasonable criticism must not be construed as defiance and nullification. We need an intelligent and understanding attitude by those outside the South who are concerned with our problem. More depends however on work at the local level. Participation by outsiders at the present moment, even by those from adjoining county, causing some trouble.

Appointment of official State and local committees which include both races would be great help. Problem not too great for solution if consultation encouraged and strengthened faith in the South's intellectual and moral resources is displayed at this crucial state. Supreme Court decisions should be studied widely and clarifying interpretations should be sought by responsible officials. Above all, common sense should prevail and in my judgment any effort to fan fires of hatred will be sharply rebuked. We have enough trouble in the world already. Church leaders of both races are in admirable position to use influence for minimum demands of justice while stressing the necessity for preserving bridge of understanding between the groups.

That the Southern declaration did not necessarily do violence to this bridge of understanding was supported by a statement of President Eisenhower, issued when he was asked at a White House press conference what he thought his executive responsibility was in this connection:

Now, the first thing about the manifesto is this: That they say they are going to use every legal means. No one in any responsible position anywhere has talked nullification because—and there would be a place where we get to a very bad spot for the simple reason I am sworn to defend and uphold the Constitution of the United States and, of course, I can never abandon or refuse to carry out my own duty. . . .

We are not talking here about coercing, using force to, in a general way; we are simply going to uphold the Constitution of the United States, see that the progress made as ordered by the [Supreme] Court is carried out.

Now let us remember this one thing, and it is very important: The people who have this deep emotional reaction on the other side were not acting over these past three generations in defiance of the law. They were acting in compliance with the law as interpreted by the Supreme Court under the decision of 1896.

Now, that has been completely reversed, and it is going to take time for them to adjust their thinking and their progress to that. But I have never yet given up my belief that the American people, faced with a great problem like this, will approach it intelligently and with patience and with understanding, and we will get somewhere; and I do deplore any great extreme action on either side.

The *Arkansas Gazette* indicated that our declaration strongly reflected the sentiment of the great majority of the people of this state, that it was a "sober and reasoned statement," and that it "offered some sound advice to the South by warning against violence and against the provocations of agitators." I was pleased to note that the *Gazette* found it significant that the Southern senators and congressmen "limited their statement to 'a declaration of constitutional principles' and did not ally themselves with any nullification or interposition movement," and that they did not "recommend any specific means of contesting the Supreme Court's anti-segregation ruling." As the *Gazette* put it, "The Washington statement will not meet with the approval of extremists on either side—of individuals or organizations with closed minds and inflexible programs. But the Southern senators and representatives have appealed to reason and have based their appeal on facts that exist in judicial and social history in this country."

When the Powell amendment to the school construction bill was approved by the House of Representatives, I was forced to vote against the entire bill because of my convictions on the desegregation issue. Defeat of this legislation was a tragic rebuff to those of us who worked hard to increase the amount of money available for additional classrooms throughout the nation, but the Powell amendment gave us no choice. Its provisions made the federal Office of Education the judge of whether a school district was complying with the Supreme Court's desegregation decision. Such a procedure would have opened the door for intrusions into the conduct and control of our state educational system. No longer could the bill be regarded merely as a financial measure to improve our school facilities, but rather it became another step in federal domination of local governments. No one who believed as strongly as I in our system of federalism could then vote for this measure.

During this period, I felt more strongly than ever the force of Sir Henry Maine's dictum that social opinion must be in advance of the law. At about this time Miss Dorothy Thompson ably restated it when she said that "if law does not have the voluntary consent of a large majority, it cannot be enforced except by procedures that violate the principle of consent and hence the basis of the state. Law can be enforced against individual lawbreakers by indictment, arraignment and trial. But laws cannot be enforced against a nation, state, or community."

My own experience had made me increasingly aware that the "separate and equal" doctrine of *Plessy v. Ferguson*—in its original rigidity, at any rate—was out of date. Yet I felt that the 1954 decision erred seriously in throwing it out completely. There had been the possibility of a decision by the Court that could have bridged the Southern traditions, now solidified under the protection of the Plessy doctrine, and the requirements of the twentieth-century world. Even the Attorney General's brief in support of the government's case for enforced integration made an interesting admission when it said that "the Plessy case plainly does not preclude a district court from finding . . . that segregation can and in a particular case does produce unequal and inferior treatment." A great deal could have been done, working through individual localities, to reduce gradually the area of segregation in the schools without the complete repudiation of the Plessy doctrine.

It also seemed unfortunate that the 1954 decision had to rest so largely on the findings of social science rather than on legal foundations. My agreement with Benjamin Cardozo, the distinguished justice, was complete in believing that sociology could offer guidance to the law but that this was not the strongest basis for legal decisions. He equated the method of sociology with public policy and cited English law to the effect that "a series of decisions based on the grounds of public policy, however eminent the justices by whom they were delivered, cannot possess the same binding authority as decisions which deal with and formulate principles that are purely legal."

As for the right to criticize the Court, there could not be any doubt of it. Most of the country's greatest leaders had exercised that right to the utmost—and none more so than Abraham Lincoln with respect to the Dred Scott decision. Senator Ervin put it in a more humorous way when he told of an incident that occurred when he was a judge. After the sheriff told him that an attorney had been quite contemptuous of a recent decision of his, he asked if the attorney had lost his case. When told that the attorney had, Judge Ervin commented, "When a fellow loses a case, he's entitled to cuss the court for a reasonable time." Nevertheless, I never strayed from my settled conviction that the national government was pre-eminent and that the Supreme Court was the final judge of what the Constitution meant. The South would have to meet the challenge presented by the decision, within the limitations of the available means of lawful protest or demands for revision. In the spring of 1956 I prepared a speech for delivery on the floor of the House, expressing my sentiments. Its concluding paragraphs sum up my ideas as to what needed to be done:

In the light of the Supreme Court decisions, we must move toward a high degree of mutual trust in the integrity of the two functions of the government, both Federal and State. The decision of May, 1954, must be accepted as a constitutional landmark, however imperfect it may be. If it could be interpreted in terms of a doctrine of "permissive integration," we could then move forward in terms of local decision-making. The Supreme Court has forbidden the use of governmental power to enforce segregation in our school systems, and we must now also protest against those who want to enforce immediate integration. While Senator Ervin, in a *Look* magazine statement, April 3, 1956, sees a possible answer in "voluntary school segregation," I should rather look at the solution in a more positive sense, permitting gradual integration, this "permissive integration," in communities where social opinion has become amenable to this development. We could then progress step by step in conformance with the wishes of each local community, and yet provide the setting for reconciliation with the rulings of the Court. The most fundamental development underlying this advance is the "education" of our people. So also the Negro must be prepared to take advantage of the opportunities to be offered him. It is no evidence at all of a lack of benevolence or humanitarian interest in the Negro on the part of the white majority that those opportunities were somewhat limited in the past. We must take cognizance of the facts of life as they are in the South and rely heavily on the strength of the South's intellectual and moral resources in our future programming.

William Faulkner expressed the firm feelings of the moderate Southerner when he concluded a *Life* magazine statement, March 5, 1956, in this way: "So I would say to all organizations and groups which would force integration on the South by legal process: 'Stop now for a moment. You have shown the Southerner what you can do and what you will do if necessary. Give him a space in which to get his breath and assimilate that knowledge; to look about and see that (1) nobody is going to force integration on him from the outside; (2) he himself faces an obsolescence in his own land which only he can cure; a moral condition which not only must be cured but a physical condition which has got to be cured if he, the white Southerner, is to have any peace, is not to be faced with another legal process or maneuver every year, year after year, for the rest of his life.' "

CHAPTER FIVE

Civil Rights in Convention and Congress

PRESIDENT EISENHOWER HAD PLEDGED, IN HIS 1956 STATE OF the Union message, that he would recommend setting up a bipartisan study commission to investigate complaints of infringements of civil rights. Based on this pledge, the Attorney General submitted to the Congress on April 9, 1956, the administration's civil rights program. In summary, it called for the following: (1) creation of a six-member bipartisan civil rights commission named by the President and confirmed by the Senate. It would investigate denials of voting rights and "unwarranted economic pressures" based on color, race, religion, or national origin, utilizing the subpoena power (recommended by President Truman's Committee on Civil Rights); (2) establishment of an additional Assistant Attorney General in the Department of Justice in charge of a new Civil Rights Division (to replace the Civil Rights Section in the Criminal Division), responsible for enforcement of the civil rights statutes (also recommended by President Truman in his 1948 Civil Rights message); (3) broadening of the statutes which now apply only to state and local officials, to permit federal prosecution of the private individuals who intimidate voters in an election for federal office; (4) authority for the Attorney General to bring civil injunction proceedings in behalf of an aggrieved individual; (5) authority for any private citizen to complain to a federal court in relation to a civil rights denial, without first going through state courts; (6) authority for the Attorney General to initiate civil actions against civil rights conspiracies, such as threats against federal grand jury or trial jury witnesses, or the use of hoods or other disguises to deprive any citizen of equal treatment under the law.

This new proposal, introduced as H.R. 627, was approved by the House Judiciary Committee (after it had rejected a still stronger program recommended by Congressman Celler of N.Y.) and then brought to the floor of the House. Before it was debated, however, Democratic Representative Tuck, former Virginia governor, circulated a resolution objecting to the provisions of this bill. I signed this resolution along with eighty-two other members of the House, although I later indicated some reservations about its contents. The following excerpts indicate its message and tone:

The bill authorizes the Commission, with the aid of paid investigators and "voluntary" pressure groups and professional informers, to launch a sweeping "investigation of allegations" which might lead them to believe that "unwarranted economic pressure" is supposedly being exerted by private individuals over others, because of their religion as well as their race. In addition and wholly unrelated to race or religion, the Commission is directed to "study and collect information concerning economic, social and legal developments" and "to appraise the laws and policies of the Federal Government" in the entire field of so-called civil rights. The term "civil rights" itself is not defined; and what would constitute unwarranted pressure, economic, social, and legal developments, and the scope of the appraisal and investigation, are left to the whim of the Commission.

. . . A politically minded Attorney General could subject the governments of States, counties, towns and localities and the officials and citizens of the same to insults, intimidation, and terror, against which there would be no redress.

Armed with the power which this legislation would expressly confer, the Attorney General, even without the consent of the plaintiffs, could file purely private law suits by and for private citizens against their neighbors. In no case would it be necessary to prove the commission of any overt act, and under the bill the Attorney General could obtain an injunction on the simple allegation that the defendant "is about to engage in an attempt" to do something that the lawyers in the Civil Rights Division conceive to be objectionable. All actions would be filed in the Federal Courts and tried without a jury, and Congress, for the first time in history, would specifically permit the Attorney General to bypass State law and ignore available local remedy. . . .

The broad language of the bill would open practically the entire field of elections, including State primaries, to Federal intervention. The intrusion of the Federal Government into this field has not heretofore been permitted or even considered, except in precise instances clearly defined by the Fourteenth and Fifteenth Amendments. If additional powers in matters of elections are deemed to be necessary to be vested in the Federal Government, then Congress should attack the problem squarely by proposing an amendment to the Constitution.

While I was in sympathy with much of this resolution, my concern over its general tenor and the use of such words as "sinister" and "iniquitous" led me to issue a statement to the press clarifying my position as follows:

I have joined in the statement condemning the so-called civil rights bill because it is contrary to convictions which I have held throughout my life with reference to Constitutional powers of the Federal and State governments. The right to vote along with many other precious rights must be protected, but the States are the best guardians of these rights. There was real wisdom in the decision of the framers of our Federal Constitution to leave election procedures to the States. Whenever the Government has departed from this fundamental principle, as in the tragic Reconstruction period, the consequences carried an impressive lesson. The lesson should be heeded now, but the issue should not be identified with questions of race. It has nothing whatever to do with the Supreme Court decisions requiring desegregation of public schools, and it is unfortunate that the civil rights statement is being construed by some as having this implication. I have demonstrated by my advocacy of reforms in election laws of Arkansas that I believe the right of franchise is sacred.

This conception of State responsibility carries with it, naturally, a continuing opposition to unwarranted invasion by Federal authority of control over elections. This is a period in which we should exert ourselves to avoid misunderstandings between racial groups. Those who would exploit any differences between them are rendering a great disservice.

While I am convinced that the exalted language and lofty sentiments of the proponents of this civil rights bill were genuine and sincere, they did not disguise the fact that this was force legislation. We would do well to consider this measure from the standpoint of human relations rather than legal technicalities, and then we would find that it provided the dangerous precedent of projecting the federal government, as a protagonist, into the area of community relationships. We could not expect a community to bow to federal dictation unless the conditions necessary for general acceptance were present. I pointed out again and again to my colleagues that no law would ever be effective unless the basis for compliance was laid in the sentiments of the people affected by it, and here there was constant work for the churches, the civil associations, and all the voluntary organizations that made up our complex democratic life.

The wide-sweeping responsibilities placed in the hands of the Attorney General in this proposal were certainly not warranted by developments in many areas of the governmental process. It is indeed ironic that the civil rights issue should have led to suggested intrusions into the realm of states' rights, when all other Congressional efforts were designed to encourage more state control of its assigned functions. The provision of the bill which would have permitted the Attorney General to act without the litigant's exhausting administrative and state court remedies or even without the private person's bringing suit at all was obviously to be understood as a vote of no confidence in state legal systems. When the justification was that "otherwise the Government is forced to rely on the uncertainties of enforcement by private litigants," we were faced with an effort to change our entire legal system, which is predicated on the development of law by individual cases and which does not condone government interference with private appeals.

Despite these objections, the civil rights bill passed the House by a large margin. It died, however, in the Senate Judiciary Committee during the rush to end the session of Congress just before the presidential conventions in August of 1956. It may be said that many members of the House voted for the measure, knowing full well that it was going to be killed in the Senate. Members of both parties attempted to make political capital of their support of civil rights in an election year, attempting to win the Negro vote in the North without actually granting the Negro any additional rights. It was in this atmosphere that Democrats assembled in Chicago in August, 1956, to write a platform and choose a presidential candidate.

Much had been going on, however, to offset the dangerous rumblings of a party fight. Because of the success we had enjoyed in our preconvention conversations in Washington in 1952, the Democratic National Committee believed we could also prevent a repetition of the 1948 experience this time by creating a similar committee. In the spring of 1956,

Paul Butler convened several informal meetings; as chairman of the Democratic party he was determined that the party should state a position on civil rights that would not be disruptive, yet would represent no retreat from the positions we had maintained in the past. Unapologetically, he sought the opinions of Southern constituencies as well as those of the well organized minority civil-rights-conscious groups in other regions, such as the NAACP and the ADA. (This practice of asking help in drafting planks was extended to other fields and was particularly effective in dealing with the foreign policy problems.)

Mr. Butler was handicapped by the necessity at that stage of avoiding publicity, for his work was something that would have been a fine target for the opposition; he was further handicapped by the fact that not everyone whose views were essential to a successful handling of the problem could be in Washington for such discussions. He took advantage of Mrs. Franklin D. Roosevelt's occasional trips to the capital to get her reactions to the work being done. He also made sure, through his innumerable contacts, that the suggested platform statements with alternative phrasing were kept truly representative. Among those who helped him in these discussions in Washington were Senator Sam Ervin of North Carolina, former Governor John Battle of Virginia, and I—all from states then in sympathy with "moderation." From "the other side" were Senator John Pastore of Rhode Island and Congressman William L. Dawson of Illinois (whose fourteen years in Congress and life-long devotion to the interests of his fellow American Negroes gave him a valid claim to confidence as a spokesman for Negro Democrats). Paul Butler's staff, Clayton Fritchey and Philip Stern, did some very effective work. They sat with us and provided excellent craftsmanship in getting into concise language the things that we agreed upon. My participation in this preliminary drafting was, of course, with the full knowledge and approval of Speaker Rayburn who had often discussed these civil rights problems with me.

This advisory subcommittee was able to compose its differences in a spirit of harmony and cooperation. Despite the many difficult problems which had arisen since 1952, particularly those created by the 1954 and 1955 Supreme Court decisions outlawing segregation, our group was able to agree on language guaranteeing the individual rights and liberties of all Americans. Everyone was anxious to preserve the unity of the Democratic party, and doctrinaire positions were reconciled through the good will efforts of the participants. Most of the drafting work was accomplished at two meetings held at the Sheraton Carlton Hotel in the room of Paul Butler, the first on July 20 and the second on July 28. We were now prepared to go to Chicago with a plank that should win party approval and gain national acceptance. Our major concern was to keep extremists on both sides from upsetting the applecart by carrying the fight to the Convention floor. While we hoped to keep the results of our work confidential to avoid an early open break, the inevitable happened—a few days before the Convention began, the *New York Times* obtained a copy of our outline and published it on August 10. It was an essentially correct reproduction (with minor differences) of our own final working paper to be laid before the platform drafting subcommittee, and it read as follows:

Every American child irrespective of race or national origin, economic status or place of residence, has full rights under the law without discrimination to every educational opportunity to develop his potentialities. [This was actually intended to be placed in the General Welfare section, under the subtitle "Education."]

The Democratic Party is dedicated to full recognition and protection of the individual rights and liberties of all Americans.

The basic concept of our governmental system is that all men are created free and equal, are entitled to all political rights and all opportunities for education, employment, and decent living conditions without discrimination.

The Democratic Party has provided the greatest advancement in the area of human rights and in the elimination of discrimination based on race, religion, or national origin. Democratic Administrations took the first concrete actions to eliminate segregation in the armed forces, to end discrimination in Government employment and to appoint qualified persons of all races to high Government posts; to ban discrimination by Government employment facilities in the nation's capital.

The Republican Administration, on the other hand, has promised much and boasted much but has done little. Words are no substitute for deeds. What is required is cooperative effort on the part of individual citizens as well as action of local, state, and Federal governments.

Americans acting individually and through governmental agencies must recognize the principle enunciated in the Declaration of Independence. The Government must exercise the powers vested in it by the Constitution and laws of the land.

We advocate Federal legislation (1) to secure the right to equal opportunity for employment, (2) to provide protection for the right to security of person, (3) to protect all citizens in the exercise of their rights, (4) to perfect and strengthen existing Federal civil rights law, (5) to provide effective administrative machinery for the protection of civil rights.

According to the *Times,* this proposed plank was being circulated by influential members of the Committee on Platform and Resolutions of the Democratic National Convention. Of course, no official cognizance was taken of this "leak," but we were forced to take even greater precautions to prevent the press from getting further confidential information. We were hopeful that compromises could still be achieved, provided the Platform Committee members were not placed in the public spotlight too soon. Much depended on the "timing" of our efforts to preserve harmony.

Meanwhile, during the Platform Committee hearings and deliberations in Chicago on the week of August 6 (one week before the Convention began), it became apparent that the platform provisions were intimately involved with the candidacies of Adlai Stevenson and Averell Harriman for the Democratic nomination. In the main, Southern delegates were disposed to stay in the Democratic party and fight out their battles there, if any sort of acceptable compromise could be worked out. For months before this, responsible Democratic leaders in the South, despite the Congressional and judicial disputes over civil rights, had been holding in check the talk of a third party. They were mindful, however, of what an extreme civil rights plank would mean to the people of their region. As one of the prominent Southern delegates said, "We'll stay in the Democratic Party. There'll be no bolt, provided we have a 'moderate' platform and a 'moderate' candidate." Thus the platform and the candidate were being fitted together into one package, with "moderation" the keynote for advocates of a civil rights plank similar to that of 1952 and for supporters of a candidate such as Adlai Stevenson for the presidency.

The supporters of Averell Harriman were convinced of the need for a plank on civil rights that gave complete approval to the Supreme Court decisions on school integration and called for language explicitly recognizing the Court's authority in this area. Mr. Harriman continued to belabor Mr. Stevenson because the latter had put himself on the side of "moderation." Some Northern liberals were complaining that the Democratic party was compromising away its principles, based on the New Deal and the Fair Deal, and asserted that Mr. Harriman was the only standard-bearer available who could champion the true cause. Those of us who had worked on the original civil rights statement held our breath, hoping that these cries would not upset the results of our prolonged negotiations before approval was gained from the full Committee and the Convention delegates.

It was at this time that Mr. Stevenson exploded his bombshell on a television program, when he commented: "I've had a very strong feeling that the platform should express unequivocal approval of the Court's decisions, although it seems odd that you have to express your approval of the Constitution and its institutions." Understandably, this caused an uproar among Adlai's Southern supporters and threatened for awhile to break down the delicate accord achieved originally in Washington. After this Stevenson statement identifying himself with the Northern liberals, his backers immediately set out to soothe Southern feelings and gave assurance that his attitude was still moderate.

Congressman John McCormack had again accepted the chairmanship of the Democratic Platform Committee, this time unwillingly, but with the fervent desire to steer the party through the rough waters of civil rights controversy. In order to achieve a conciliatory spirit, he put himself in charge of the seventeen-member platform-writing subcommittee which was to consider the civil rights plank originally prepared by the Washington conference team. Harry Truman offered this advice to the subcommittee: write a platform that is "very specific and plain," but above all write "a platform on which we can win in November." The Southern role at this time was mainly concerned with keeping out of the plank any clear endorsement of the Supreme Court school rulings and also keeping out any threat of "force" to back up these rulings. It was also distasteful to the South to accept the section on general welfare, which upheld "full rights under the law, without discrimination, to every educational opportunity . . . for every American child."

While the hearings were being held on the various planks of the platform, I left my campaign for re-election to Congress several days in advance of the primary election (equivalent to election in my district) to travel to Chicago at the request of the party leadership. I participated in the early discussions of the civil rights plank and did what I could to support the preliminary draft which Mrs. Roosevelt, Mr. Dawson, Mr. Pastore, Mr. Battle, Mr. Ervin, and I had prepared. I took this opportunity to visit with Adlai Stevenson and to plead that he hold the party together. I told him of the strains we faced in holding the two major factions together and asked that he bear with those Southern moderates who were anxious to support him if he did not make such a position untenable. He was not as unbending as some of the civil rights "purists"; however, he was not as yielding as party professionals would have preferred.

At the same time, I reassured Mr. Stevenson concerning the strength of his Southern support, since this was just after he had announced that he favored a platform declaration approving the Supreme Court decisions, and it was considered that his Southern delegates were, as one of his managers phrased it, "climbing the wall." I told him about my meeting with Negro leaders in Little Rock after signing the "Manifesto" and before my primary election. Since my record had been friendly to the minority race and I had striven to promote their progress, I had always had a firm hold on Negro voters in the past. Now they were virtually unanimous in condemning all of the Southern congressmen who attacked the Supreme Court rulings. I was surprised, however, when an old friend, Dr. T. W. Coggs, former president of a Negro college, addressed the gathering as follows: "Our people are critical of you for signing [the Manifesto], but not many will desert you. I say to them that they should judge you on your whole record which is good, not on a single action." Then he related the story of a funeral sermon which he said had been used effectively in my defense to illustrate the point. The minister was using a bit of drama to emphasize the point that all was well with the soul of a departed member—a good woman who was being taken to heaven "by the planetary route." Dr. Coggs said that the congregation was eagerly following the transition. "He got her to Mars, then to Venus, but somewhere up there around Saturn he seemed to lose her and the members became nervous." One deacon excitedly called out, "Find her, Brother Bill, find her," but he was calmed by another deacon. "Oh, he'll find her all right. I've seen him lose 'em and find 'em before." Said Dr. Coggs: "I just tell my people that I've seen you slip before and then get back on the right track."

Mr. Stevenson was delighted with this story—he buried his head in his hands and repeated, as if he were already planning to use it, "I've seen him lose 'em and find 'em before." In the course of this conversation with Adlai, I sensed a deep personal conviction to accord the Negro people their full rights, and I was convinced that expediency did not dictate his decision to speak more clearly on the point than we of the Platform Committee were planning to speak. However, his position complicated our task, and we were a bit upset by it from the standpoint of winding up our civil rights statement without friction.

In my conversation with Adlai on that Saturday before the Convention opened, I was able to convey to him some sidelights of the political dilemmas that faced the Southern moderate at that time. I asked him to distinguish between those who advocated nullification and interposition and those who presented honest criticisms of the 1954 decisions.

It was precisely because Southern people were devoted to the rule of law that they deplored the attempts to convert the decision's phrase "deliberate speed" into "majestic instancy," as contemplated in the many lawsuits being filed in the region. I pointed out to Adlai that it would be difficult to dispose of the question in a simple platform commitment to carry out the decision without also recognizing the valid principle that criticism of judicial decisions is a cherished American right, even though it was now being exercised by those who preferred the old order.

He was impressed by my reference to the Little Rock conference with Negro church leaders in which I had pleaded for patience with those of us who regard the time factor as the key to real progress for their race. I gently had reminded them that the right to condemn a Supreme Court decision is the very thing that enabled them to gain the judicial advantage they now hold. I reported to Adlai what I had then said to my Negro friends: "It was not un-American of you to attack the separate-but-equal [*Plessy v. Ferguson*] decision of 1896, and for at least thirty years you have been doing that. It is only when criticism and efforts for clarification are joined with defiance that the dissenters are guilty of weakening our judicial structure in which both groups have such a vital stake. Your gains have been made by attacking the legal sanctions for discrimination." Adlai nodded and said: "I hadn't thought of that." He was also impressed by my acknowledgement of the significance of the "scolding" which the colored ministers had given me. (The full details of this Little Rock meeting are given in a following chapter.)

I assured Adlai that we Southerners on the Platform Committee were Stevenson men, but we foresaw that we would pay a price in loss of Southern votes by maintaining an unbending position. Undoubtedly he was aware that he had everything to lose and Governor Harriman had everything to gain should a floor fight develop on civil rights. (The New York Governor's strategists figured their man had no broad Southern support to lose by his strong civil rights advocacy, and it could only help him among Northerners who agreed with his stand.) My conversation with Mr. Stevenson made me hopeful that he would do nothing to drive out of his camp the Southern moderates who saw in his candidacy the best hope for the preservation of the ideals for which the Democratic party has long stood. I also left his room with greater determination to work for a civil rights plank that would both do justice to this man who, I was convinced, would be our presidential nominee and at the same time not be an affront to Southern people who must continue to struggle with problems of implementation.

The endorsement of Averell Harriman by Harry Truman at this moment, on the eve of the Convention (Saturday, August 11), served to goad the Stevenson forces to head off the development of a "dark horse" compromise candidate. This meant that Adlai Stevenson would be under greater pressure from his campaign managers not to jeopardize his chances for the nomination by making any rash statements between Saturday and the Convention consideration of the proposed platform on Wednesday evening. Most of the leaders of ADA were supporting Mr. Harriman, but he failed to gain the necessary breadth of support to make him a real contender. The Harriman men, frustrated and losing strength at every turn, threw their efforts into a last-ditch drive for a more emphatic declaration on civil rights in the platform. Nonetheless, the forces of moderation still believed they had a good chance to carry the day.

After a long and arduous struggle, a plank was written by the platform subcommittee that was deemed acceptable to both Northern liberals and Southern conservatives. The vote was twelve to five, with the five Southerners on the subcommittee casting "No" votes in what was described by several persons as a "token protest for the record." Besides myself, this five-man group included Governor J. P. Coleman of Mississippi, Senator Sam Ervin of North Carolina, former Governor John S. Battle of Virginia, and Vann H. Kennedy of Texas. Although we were concerned that many Southern voters might be alarmed by some of the things the platform said, we did not deem them crippling to the Southern position. The subcommittee refused to circulate its statement until just before the full Committee was to meet, to avoid further "leaks" to the press and to permit the presidential nomination picture to become somewhat clarified— a crucial development related to platform approval by the Convention. While the language was not revealed, Senator Ervin and Governor Battle felt it necessary to make clear that they had made great concessions to the majority. It was thus understood that no opposition would be forthcoming from the South if the Convention accepted the present wording. A rugged fight was threatened, however, if the plank were changed to give specific support to the Supreme Court's desegregation decisions. This was an obvious indication that the plank was "softpedaling" on the words "Supreme Court" and on enforcement language.

During the debate, Representative Emanuel Celler of New York offered several amendments to "strengthen" the plank in accord with the wishes of the "strong" civil rights proponents, but he was shouted down, and ultimately agreed to vote for the majority plank in the interest of party unity. The others who voted for this wording were Chairman McCormack, Miss Grace Hudlin of Oklahoma, Mrs. Emma Guffey Miller of Pennsylvania, Representative Gracie Pfost of Idaho, Representative Dawson of Illinois, former Governor Paul Dever of Massachusetts, Senator Theodore Francis

Green of Rhode Island, Representative John Moss of California, Senator Joseph C. O'Mahoney of Wyoming, former Representative Jennings Randolph of West Virginia, and Mrs. Thelma Parkinson Sharp of New Jersey. After he left the session, Congressman Celler said: "This is an extremely liberal platform, the most liberal platform that the Democratic party has adopted in my experience. I voted for it and I will support it." This attitude on the part of Mr. Celler made me confident of our position before the Convention and I was quoted as saying: "I think there is a fighting chance to get it through the full Committee without a minority report from either side."

The only note of discord was sounded by Charles Diggs, Jr., Negro Representative from Michigan, who claimed he had more than the required eleven votes to file a minority report from the 108-member full Platform Committee should he feel one necessary. We could only hope that he could be dissuaded from coming up with such a report demanding specific platform support of the Supreme Court school decisions.

Some indication of the value of this Convention's preparatory discussions was the speed with which the drafting committee dealt with the civil rights plank. In 1952, most of the night was taken for the same job which was accomplished by this subcommittee in two and a half hours. Most of the committee members had been fully briefed on the problems involved, and the disagreements had been ironed out well in advance of the actual Convention meetings.

Our next hurdle was the meetings of the full 108-member Platform Committee in its tower sanctuary at the Conrad Hilton Hotel. These meetings ran right up to the time of the platform presentation to the Convention. At first, there was little discussion of the provisions of the civil rights plank. Congressman Diggs and Mr. Belford V. Lawson of the District of Columbia raised some questions but seemed to be mollified by the answers they received. When one of the Oregon members of the Committee moved the previous question, he was asked to hold his motion in abeyance for awhile to permit free discussion. Shortly thereafter, the platform was accepted *without a dissenting vote*. A motion to reconsider was laid on the table, and it appeared that we had escaped the possibility of a minority report. Here is how the civil rights plank read:

The Democratic party is committed to support and advance the individual rights and liberties of all Americans. Our country is founded on the proposition that all men are created equal. This means that all citizens are equal before the law and should enjoy equal political rights. They should have equal opportunities for education, for economic advancement, and for decent living conditions.

We will continue our efforts to eradicate discrimination based on race, religion or national origin. We know this task requires action, not just in one section of the nation, but in all sections. It requires the cooperative efforts of individual citizens, and action by state and local governments. It also requires federal action. The federal government must live up to the ideals of the Declaration of Independence and must exercise the powers vested in it by the Constitution.

We are proud of the record of the Democratic party in securing equality of treatment and opportunity in the nation's armed forces, the Civil Service, and in all areas under federal jurisdiction. The Democratic party pledges itself to continue its efforts to eliminate illegal discriminations of all kinds in relation to (1) full rights to vote, (2) full rights to engage in gainful occupations, (3) full rights to enjoy security of the person, and (4) full rights to education in publicly supported institutions.

Recent decisions of the Supreme Court of the United States relating to segregation in publicly supported schools and elsewhere have brought consequences of vast importance to our nation as a whole and especially to communities directly affected. We reject all proposals for the use of force to interfere with the orderly determination of these matters by the courts.

The Democratic party emphatically reaffirms its support of the historic principles that ours is a government of laws and not of men; it recognizes the Supreme Court of the United States as one of the three constitutional and coordinate branches of the federal government, superior to and separate from any political party, the decisions of which are part of the law of the land. We condemn the efforts of the Republican party to make it appear that this tribunal is a part of the Republican party.

We condemn the Republican Administration's violation of the rights of government employees by a heartless and unjustified confusing of "security" and "loyalty" for the sole purpose of political gain and regardless of consequences to individual victims and of the good name of the United States. We condemn the Republican Administration's misrepresentation of facts and violation of individual rights in a wicked and unprincipled attempt to degrade and destroy the Democratic party, and to make political capital for the Republican party.

The Supreme Court decisions were referred to as having "brought consequences of vast importance to our nation as a whole and especially to communities directly affected." In accord with Southern wishes, the plank committed the Democratic party to "reject all proposals for the use of force to interfere with the orderly determination of these matters by the courts." Then the plan, in deference to the North, went on to say that "the Democratic party ... recognizes the Supreme Court of the United States as one of the three constitutional and coordinate branches of the federal government, superior to and separate from any political party, the decisions of which are part of the law of the land." The general welfare plank retained the paragraph on education upholding the right of every child, "irrespective of race or national origin, economic status or place of residence ... to

every educational opportunity for developing his potentialities" without being discriminated against. The same paragraph was contained in the 1952 plank on education, but no
mention was made then of the phrase "without discrimination." In balance, I think it is fair to say that each side made
real concessions in order to meet the demands of the other
and still secure the minimal standards of justice.

When such people as Governor Leader of Pennsylvania
and other Northern governors, mayors, and political leaders
saw the plank, an uproar occurred. Prodded by the NAACP
and the ADA, they demanded significant changes in the
wording to support more explicitly the Supreme Court school
decisions and generally repeat a key paragraph of the 1952
plank. When Congressman Diggs explained to me the need
for a new meeting of the Platform Committee, I understood
that this pressure for more positive language was a genuine
voicing of aspirations not to be ignored. In this regard I differed from my Southern brethren, some of whom referred to
this liberal group as "party subversives." While I disagreed
completely with the aims of the "extremists," they were to be
respected for being true to their principles. It became my lot
to try to maintain the role of "bridge-builder" between the
two rival groups.

It was still the anxious wish of those of us who had
steered the moderate plank through the Platform Committee to avoid a floor fight on civil rights. Former Governor
Dever of Massachusetts, who had done such an admirable
job in contributing to the cooperative atmosphere on the
Committee, joined with Congressman McCormack and me
in suggesting a re-referral of the plank to a "committee of
six" to iron out existing differences. Senator Ervin said,
"Nothing doing," trembling with anger at the suggestion
of a revival of the whole issue. He believed that he had done
all in his power to prepare a plank acceptable to North and

South, and that he could not tolerate any further concessions to the North. He even went so far as to blame the
Stevenson forces for the move for re-assessment. The situation appeared to be deteriorating, and all the diplomacy and
good will available were necessary to save the day.

Anna Rosenberg, Thomas Finletter, Senator Herbert Lehman, Jacob Arvey, David Lawrence, and Robert Nathan
gathered to formulate the precise language they wished to
have added to the existing wording of the plank. In the
fourth paragraph they wanted the clause "We pledge to
carry out those decisions, but" to be inserted before the
sentence beginning "We reject all proposals for the use of
force. . . ." They also suggested the inclusion of the same
paragraph which had closed the 1952 plank, as follows: "At
the same time we favor Federal legislation effectively to
secure these rights to everyone: (1) the right to equal opportunity for employment; (2) the right to security of persons; (3) the right to full and equal participation in the Nation's political life, free from arbitrary restraints. We also
favor legislation to perfect existing Federal civil rights statutes and to strengthen the administrative machinery for the
protection of civil rights." Curiously enough, these liberals
were advocating the acceptance of legislation "effectively to
secure these rights," when it was the word "effectively" in
the 1952 plank which had appealed to Southerners. They
had argued then that some Northern proposals were not
effective and therefore not significant in carrying out the
intended purposes. I point this out only to show how complicated the drawing up of a platform can be and how difficult it is to avoid using language that means one thing to
one group and another thing to another group. We now faced
the problem of meeting these new demands, based on language not clearly understood by either its proponents or its
opponents.

It became my function to serve as a bridge between Mrs. Rosenberg and Congressman McCormack. She made it clear that she would be willing to give up the struggle on the controversial paragraph provided the still more controversial "we pledge to carry out these decisions" was accepted in the plank. This was obviously completely unacceptable to the South. The Alabama and Georgia Platform Committee members made clear their unequivocal opposition to the previously mentioned compromise proposal to set up a six-man committee to study the problem. At a hastily called meeting of the Platform Committee, this motion failed and the meeting adjourned with no resolution of the conflict. I was unable to bring the viewpoint of Mrs. Rosenberg into a form acceptable to Mr. McCormack's needs, and we were faced with the inevitability of a floor fight over the minority proposal.

The Convention had not begun its Wednesday evening session until long past the scheduled time because of this acrimonious off-the-floor debate. On the floor itself, starting at about 8:00 P.M., there was much evidence of conflict and bitterness. For example, Congressman Jimmy Roosevelt informed his California delegation that the civil rights plank approved by the "unanimous" Platform Committee was "no good at all." A general uproar was taking possession of the Convention Hall and Chairman Rayburn, outraged, bellowed: "Delegates will cease walking and talking or retire from the Chamber!" Internal differences were evident in state delegation after state delegation, with Steve Mitchell feuding with Senator Paul Douglas of Illinois, and various other delegates bickering over details of the platform.

Meanwhile, John McCormack and I were meeting with Jim Finnegan, Paul Butler, Jake Arvey, and Carmine De-Sapio in a last-ditch effort to find suitable language for a unanimous report. I proposed that paragraph three of the plank contain the sentence "We welcome all appropriate executive, legislative, and judicial support for these principles" at the end of the enumeration of the rights guaranteed. I discovered from Governor Coleman, however, that such language was unacceptable to his state at that time. If it had been included in the original draft, it might have succeeded in preventing the breach, but at this late date it would attract the kind of attention that would reflect unfavorably on the Southern delegates. On the other hand, it seemed impossible to prevent the Northern wing from continuing with its "rebel" movement. Jim Finnegan was blamed for this recalcitrance, but he met the criticism courageously and pointed out that there was little he could do to deter such men as Senator Lehman and Governor Mennen Williams. In a very difficult spot, he defended himself and Adlai Stevenson in a most professional manner and gave evidence of his political awareness and knowledge of the difficulties of the situation.

Chairman Rayburn had been kept informed of the struggle by John McCormack and now stepped in to exert his influence on the deliberations. He arranged a huddle of negotiators behind the Speaker's rostrum in a final desperate effort to work out another compromise and avert a floor fight. Such men as Mayor Daley of Chicago, Senator Douglas, and Senator Lehman joined the conference. The "Southern Five" of the Platform Drafting Committee, Messrs. Battle, Coleman, Kennedy, Ervin, and I, made an urgent plea for the Convention to stand by the platform as written. When Mr. Rayburn was told that the 1956 plank was stronger than that of 1952, he asked for a copy to read. His reaction to the statement of principles was: "This is a much better plank than we had in '52!" He was prepared to do his best to block the acceptance of a minority report on the floor, but he could not convince its advocates that they had nothing to gain. In the end, of course, it was agreed to permit the minority report to be offered and award the Northern wing time to state its case.

As the conferees strode away from their "huddle," Paul Butler told the press sadly: "It looks like there'll be a floor fight." John Battle was heard to say that, although the liberal wing had come in with a lot of amendments, "we agreed on a plank this afternoon and we're not going to change it." I then informed the reporters that "the civil rights plank is going before the Convention as it was originally written by the Platform Committee." John Mc-Cormack, in a prelude to the reading of various platform planks, declared that he was "going to fight just as hard as I can to maintain unity in the Democratic Party" by having the platform adopted as written. Introduced as platform chairman, he read the preamble to the proposed platform at about 10:30 P.M. and then in turn began introducing others to read the document's eleven planks. While speaker after speaker read other platform planks to the Convention delegates, the rival forces on the civil rights issue planned their strategy.

It was almost quiet in the hall when Chairman McCormack himself arose to read the civil rights plank, the last item of the eleven. He drew scattered applause when he read the words "Supreme Court." He ended the reading quickly and Mr. Rayburn resumed the chair. Robert Short of Minneapolis, head of the Minnesota delegation, was recognized to present the minority report, supported by fourteen Platform Committee members, three more than the necessary eleven. He then explained the liberal demand that the Democratic party pledge to carry out the decisions on school segregation of the Supreme Court. When he had finished, there was loud applause, mixed with catcalls and the waving of Rebel flags. Other liberals who rose to support him included Senator Lehman of New York, delegate Richard Richards of California, Governor Williams of Michigan, and Senator Douglas of Illinois.

When the minority case had been stated, the Northern moderates began their defense of the majority report. It was decided that Southern spokesmen should remain quiet so that national interest and party unity could be presented as the basis of the majority argument. It was still a sad commentary on the state of national understanding that no Southerner could speak in the interest of the Democratic party. Such liberals as former Governor of Massachusetts Paul Dever, Congressman Dawson, Congressman John Moss of California, and finally Congressman John McCormack rose to champion the Platform Committee's civil rights plank, emphasizing the lack of any opposition in the Platform Committee meetings themselves. Mr. McCormack made an impassioned plea for party unity and pointed out quite clearly that this plank was the strongest ever presented, because it pledged Democratic party support for (1) full rights to vote, (2) full rights to engage in gainful occupations, (3) full rights to enjoy security of person, and (4) full rights to education in publicly supported institutions, these provisions obviously making totally unnecessary the inclusion of the new paragraph advocated by the minority.

I was sitting with the Arkansas delegation during the floor debate on civil rights and noticed that members of the Michigan delegation across the aisle were making disrespectful remarks during Mr. McCormack's speech. Arkansas' Governor Faubus also was disturbed by this activity and inquired of the nearest delegate from Michigan, "Where's your sense of tolerance?" This gentleman, an auto worker from Detroit, turned around and sneered, "Aw, pipe down, you cotton-

picker!" Another member of the Arkansas delegation re-
torted, "If you steelworkers do as well as us cotton-pickers,
we'll elect a Democratic president this fall." The Governor
turned to me and commented amusedly: "He doesn't know
how little cotton I've picked—he should have said straw-
berries." This little by-play revealed the new configuration
of forces within the Democratic party and points up the
differences between the "New North" and the "New South."
We have yet to see the full significance of the changes taking place, and what the resolution of these forces in the
South will be depends upon the maintenance of a spirit of
good will and tolerance despite the occasional rebuffs.

At the conclusion of the debate from the Speaker's stand,
Mr. Rayburn, with his usual parliamentary skill, found a way
to yield the floor to non-delegate Harry Truman. Mr. Truman
rose in his box seat to state his own opinion of the platform. Since he was still championing the cause of Averell
Harriman's candidacy, it was to be expected that he would
advocate the strongest civil rights plank possible. He began
by claiming that his administration had done more to further
the recognition of the rights of minorities than any other
in our history. He then brought the Convention to its feet
cheering when he said: "I want to do something to con-
tribute harmony here. Let's get together, face the Republicans full force and give them the licking they're entitled to.
I've had a hand in every Democratic platform built since
1936. This Committee had the best chairman and the most
liberal views of any I ever saw. This is the best platform
the Party has offered since I've been working on them. Let's
adopt the majority report." The forces of moderation
breathed deep sighs of relief and felt that their long labors
had almost reached fruition.

When Sam Rayburn asked for the "yeas" and "nays" on
the acceptance of the minority civil rights plank at about

1:30 in the morning, there was a momentary hush in the auditorium. First, the "yeas" rolled forth and then the "nays." Mr. Rayburn ruled that the "nays" had it, and when cries of "no, no" went up, he silenced them quickly by declaring sternly: "I've been taking these yea and nay votes for quite a spell now and I think I know which is louder." He then asked for the "yeas" and "nays" on the acceptance of the whole platform and the "yeas" won with an overwhelming roar. The fight had been won! We had presented the party and the country with a platform that all lovers of freedom and disciples of the Declaration of Independence could embrace with pride and honor. While we did not make everyone happy, we did hold the party together behind a civil rights plank with which all factions could live.

The question may be raised as to whether a deal was made not to ask for a roll-call vote. If seven states had requested a roll call on the minority plank, the Convention would have been compelled to poll the delegations, with a very uncertain outcome. I am, of course, very pleased that no such move was made and am thankful that seven states could not be mustered to require the roll call. However, I can only say that if a deal were made, I heard nothing about it and have no knowledge of it.

In reviewing the events leading up to the acceptance of the civil rights platform, I can think of many people whose contributions were very valuable in the long and arduous process. An accolade should go to Paul Butler, who struggled in a selfless way to lay the foundations for the presentation of a unifying program. Mrs. Roosevelt performed invaluable services both in the Washington preliminary conferences and at Chicago by preventing an open breach between Northern liberals and Southern moderates. John McCormack was a tower of strength and patience throughout the negotiations and guided the deliberations with sincerity and integrity. I felt honored when he said: "Brooks, stay here with me," because I had provided him with the moral support he needed to hold him up in the darkest hours of controversy. Speaker Rayburn maneuvered the platform through the Convention with calm assurance and careful rulings. His behind-the-scenes influence extended to Harry Truman, whom he convinced to speak out in the interest of party solidarity. Last but not least, I should like to pay tribute to the representatives of the South, Governor Coleman of Mississippi, Senator Ervin of North Carolina, former Governor Battle of Virginia, and Vann Kennedy of Texas. They came to Chicago with the spirit of cooperation and kept that spirit in the face of many trials and tribulations. They were willing to concede as much as they possibly could to win Convention approval without losing the South for the Democratic party. It was this spirit, in the last analysis, that enabled us to provide the party with a clear and honest statement.

In this final form, our commitment avoided affronting any group. While there were areas of disagreement, our success in avoiding a disruptive controversy was indicative of the desire of Democrats in every part of the country to stick together and to press for Democratic victory at the polls, confident that we could put into sound legislation the basic views of our people. Without preparing a political essay, we were both concise and altogether honest in our statement of purpose. Here is what Walter Lippman had to say about our efforts:

The words of the platform are an unequivocal declaration in favor of using persuasion to bring about compliance. Insofar as the words chosen to say this are somewhat muted, are not emphatic and defiant, are couched in the language of understatement, it is because the Democratic leaders, Governor Stevenson himself and Mrs. Roosevelt, who is the keeper of the party's conscience on this issue, were wise enough not to force the hands of the Southern leaders. There are great masses of the Southern people who are not persuaded, and if they are to be persuaded, it will have to be by people who live in the South and know its problems.

For those who believe that segregation must be ended, but that it can be ended only by consent, and never by force, there is nothing weak in the civil rights plank. It is, indeed, a courageous act of accommodation on the part of the political leaders of the South, and one which does them great honor.

With the acceptance of the platform, the nomination of Adlai Stevenson was assured. While Mr. Stevenson had said he favored "specific" endorsement of the Supreme Court decisions, Southern delegates, many of whom were lawyers, viewed the language as less than an endorsement of those rulings, and, hence, acceptable if not actually pleasing. It cannot be denied that the rank and file of our citizenry might have read endorsement into it. In any event, Mr. Stevenson paid tribute to the open-mindedness of the people of Little Rock, Arkansas, when he chose it as the place to state more fully his ideas about the school integration issue in 1956. He put it this way:

The Supreme Court of the United States has determined unanimously that the Constitution does not permit segregation in the schools. As you know, for I have made my position clear on this from the start, I believe that decision to be right.

Some of you feel strongly to the contrary.

But what is most important is that we agree that once the Supreme Court has decided this constitutional question, we accept that decision as law-abiding citizens.

Our common goal is the orderly accomplishment of the result decreed by the Court. I said long ago and I stand now squarely on the plain statement, adopted in the Democratic Platform, that "we reject all proposals for the use of force to interfere with the orderly determination of these matters by the courts." The Court's decree provides for the ways and means of putting into effect the principle it sets forth. I am confident that this decision will be carried out in the manner prescribed by the courts. I have repeatedly expressed the belief, however, that the office of the Presidency should be used to bring together those of opposing views in this matter—to the end of creating a climate for peaceful acceptance of this decision.

This admirable frankness did not surprise me, and that virtue offset any disappointment his hearers experienced in listening to approval of the Supreme Court decision. It enabled his Southern followers to dispose of the charge that "in the North he makes one speech and in the South a different speech." Our answer: "Yes, the speeches are different. In the South he tells us what the nation as a whole has already decided, that is that we must live with the decision, and in the North he tells his audience that the South has problems that the North must view sympathetically."

Although Adlai Stevenson was not elected to the presidency, 1956 cannot be called a complete Democratic defeat. For the first time in our history, in the year of a presidential election, majorities in both Houses of Congress were won by the party which lost the presidential election. I firmly believe that the Democrats were able to achieve this extraordinary result because we had found a way to reconcile our differences at the Convention.

With Eisenhower elected for another term, it was to be expected that a school construction bill would again be brought up. When it came to a vote in the House in July, 1957, I was determined to support the proposal if the subject of segregation could somehow be kept from being an issue. I felt a measure of vindication for my 1956 vote when President Eisenhower made his courageous and clear-cut statement in the 1957 State of the Union message: "I am hopeful that this program can be enacted on its own merits, uncomplicated by provisions dealing with the complex problems of integration." An amendment similar to the Powell amendment had been defeated in committee but was again adopted on the floor. It had become quite evident that this so-called anti-segregation amendment was primarily designed to defeat the bill. Representative James Roosevelt and Representative Charles Diggs, both ardent supporters of civil rights, opposed the amendment on these grounds but were unable to prevent its passage.

The proponents of federal aid for schools, now fearful that the bill could not pass in its present form, decided to try another approach. The measure before the House was a Democratic proposal rather than the proposal desired by President Eisenhower. In order to gain Republican support, an attempt was made to have the President's bill substituted for the Kelley bill then being considered. This would also have meant the elimination of the segregation "rider" and made doubtful its reintroduction. Before this development could take place, however, a move was made to send the bill back to committee, essentially killing it for that session. The vote was 208 to 203 "to strike out the measure's enabling clause" or kill it. This was a tragic set-back for those of us who felt that the federal government had an obligation to help the states improve their schools. It did give me the opportunity, however, to vote for the principle of federal aid without the segregation issue being involved. It is significant that only seven Southern congressmen did vote against killing the bill, two from Arkansas and five from Alabama, indicating a general fear that the race question was too intimately involved to be kept out indefinitely. But the fact that the vote was so close gave me hope that my point of view would soon prevail with increased support from my Southern colleagues.

The most important event of this session of Congress in legislation bearing on racial problems was the final breaking of the stalemate on civil rights. The civil rights bill passed the House in essentially the same form it had in 1956. The major controversy centered around the Southern effort to have the right to trial by jury insured in cases where persons were charged with contempt of court in suits brought by the Attorney General to protect the right to vote and other civil rights. I supported this effort as a valid move to protect the Constitutional rights of accused persons. I also felt that convictions in trials by jury would be obtained where the facts were clear and that reliance on a federal judge alone would defeat the purpose of the legislation. The people of the region affected must give the law their support for it to be carried out in both the letter and the spirit, and the jury process could add immeasurably to general understanding. In any event, the attention given to cases where there were failures to convict when guilt was obvious would tend to serve as a deterrent to improper decisions. A majority of the House disagreed with me, however, and the amendment was defeated, 251-158.

In the Senate, the unusual procedure was employed of bypassing a Senate committee to have the bill placed on the Senate calendar to be called up at any time by a majority vote, in order to prevent Senator Eastland, the Chairman of the Judiciary Committee, from bottling it up. The debate centered first around Section III of the measure which gave the Attorney General power to institute proceedings to enforce the law, and this section was eliminated by a vote of fifty-two to thirty-eight. On the "jury trial" feature, an amendment was adopted to provide jury trials where defendants who had violated injunctions were charged with criminal rather than civil contempt of court. The difference between the two kinds of contempt was defined with regard to whether the defendant could purge himself of contempt by compliance with a court order (civil) or whether the sentence was inflicted for past and irremediable disobedience to an order (criminal).

I was pleased at this revision, and when the Civil Rights bill passed the Senate by a vote of seventy-two to eighteen, I hoped the House would approve the Senate version. I still did not feel that any action was necessary but told my constituents, "It might be better to have this type of legislation than risk the possibility of more extreme measures in 1958." But advocates of civil rights in the House demanded a stronger bill and rejected the establishment of a conference committee which might cause enough delay to prevent passage of any bill. Finally, with White House blessing, House Republican Leader Joe Martin suggested a complicated compromise which provided for trial by jury only when the punishment was more than ninety days in jail or a fine of $300. This compromise I could not vote for, because I believed that the guarantee of a jury trial had in effect been eliminated, although the judge's power to punish for contempt was greatly restricted. Leaders of both parties accepted the suggestion, however, and it soon became the law of the land.

We have not yet achieved the kind of compromise I have fought for since 1949, namely, a compromise between the South and other sections, not merely between the Democrats and the Republicans. Such legislation would have to take into full consideration the need for evolutionary change— not revolutionary upheaval. In this regard, we may draw some solace from the statement of Woodrow Wilson in the July, 1897, *Atlantic Monthly*: "Even the race problem of the South will no doubt work itself out in the slowness of time as blacks and whites pass from generation to generation, gaining with each remove from the memories of the war a surer self-possession, an easier view of the division of labor and of social function to be arranged between them. . . . Time is the only legislator in such a matter."

CHAPTER SIX

The Little Rock Story

IN SEPTEMBER, 1956, LITTLE ROCK WAS HERALDED AS A CITY whose plan for slow, gradual, and voluntary integration could serve as a model for many cities in the South. In an article in the *U.S. News & World Report* on September 28 of that year, entitled "How One Southern City Plans to Integrate," the pattern adopted by the Little Rock School Board was presented as a "workable compromise" likely to be accepted by both sides in the school integration dispute. Virgil T. Blossom, Superintendent of Schools, had joined his board in trying to adjust the school system in accordance with the Supreme Court's May, 1954, decision. Just six days after that decision, the board stated: "It is our responsibility to comply with Federal Constitutional requirements, and we intend to do so when the Supreme Court ... outlines the method to be followed." A rough draft of the plan that was finally accepted was completed shortly before the Court ruled that implementation of "all deliberate speed" would be left to federal district courts.

According to the plan as finally accepted, integration would take place first at the high-school level, since the smallest number of pupils would be involved and the least strain would be put on Little Rock's educational standards.

After this first step had been thoroughly tested for at least two years, junior high schools would begin this moderate integration. The last stage, involving the elementary schools, would follow another test period and the whole process would take from five to ten years to be completed. Even then, the integration that took place would be on a voluntary basis, since pupils would be permitted to transfer from one school to another.

This, then, is what Little Rock was prepared to do by September, 1957. The NAACP, early in 1956, however, after some Negroes had been refused immediate admittance to white schools, appealed to the federal courts for an order to end segregation in Little Rock. The school board presented its plan for gradual integration to Judge John E. Miller of the United States District Court in Arkansas. He approved the plan on August 28, 1956, calling it a "prompt and reasonable start" toward compliance with the Supreme Court's ruling, and praised the school board for acting "in utmost good faith." When the NAACP appealed to the U.S. Eighth Circuit Court of Appeals for reversal, the court upheld Judge Miller's decision.

This was the status of Little Rock's integration program until August of 1957. During this last month before the School Board Plan was to go into effect, forces were at work to prevent the peaceful accomplishment of this result. On August 20, Governor Faubus telephoned Governor Marvin Griffin of Georgia, who was due to address the Capital Citizens Council of Little Rock two days later. Upon being assured that Griffin and Roy Harris (former Georgia state senator and Citizens Council leader) would not make any inflammatory speeches, Governor Faubus invited them to stay at the Governor's Mansion. Said Harris later: "We had to accept Faubus' invitation to stay at the Mansion, but we had to apologize to the [Citizens] Council folks for staying there.

When we got to the airport there at Little Rock, Marv went over and greeted the Governor's delegation—the state troopers and all—and that gave me time to get to one side with *our* people. I apologized and told 'em that Marv figured it was just courtesy to accept another governor's invitation, and that being discourteous wouldn't do any good. And then I told 'em, 'Why, having us two there at the Mansion's the worse thing could happen to Faubus. It'll ruin him with the integrationists and liberals.' And they said, 'We never thought of it that way. That's fine.' "

The night of August 22, Griffin and Harris spoke at a $10 a plate dinner to raise funds to stop integration. Griffin vowed to the audience of some 350 people that he would never permit Georgia's schools to be integrated. Harris went on to say that Griffin would use the National Guard, the state patrol, and every able-bodied man in Georgia to keep the Negroes out. This development caused Governor Faubus to think twice about what he should do or not do about Little Rock's plan. The pressure was mounting for him to follow a course similar to the one advocated by Griffin. His political future might well be at stake. At the Governor's request, on August 28, 1957, A. B. Caldwell, assistant for Civil Rights in the Criminal Division of the Justice Department (and a native and former resident of Arkansas) was sent to Little Rock for a private conference. The Governor told Mr. Caldwell that he had reason to believe that there would be violence at Central High School if the Negroes tried to enter on September 3. When asked what the federal government was prepared to do if this happened, Caldwell replied that the development of a disturbance at the school would not of itself provide any basis for action by federal authorities. He made a distinction between this case and the one in Clinton, Tennessee, in which a federal court order enjoining certain people from interfering with the plan being carried out there was violated and the judge called on the assistance of the Justice Department to make the order effective.

It was in this context that a suit was filed in the Arkansas chancery court by the newly formed Mothers of Central High League to stop the implementation of the School Board Plan. On Thursday, August 29, Governor Faubus appeared before Chancellor Murray O. Reed as a witness in support of the prayer for an injunction. He testified that "violence, bloodshed and riots" would result if the integration began as scheduled and cited the increased sales of knives and revolvers to Negro and white students. While he failed to give any specific information, the chancery judge nonetheless granted the petition for an injunction.

The school board immediately appealed to the federal district court for an order prohibiting the state court from interfering with the efforts of the board to go forward with the plan. Federal Judge Ronald N. Davies, who had been sent from North Dakota to Little Rock to deal with the backlog of cases which had accumulated since Judge Trimble's retirement, heard the appeal on Friday, August 30, and issued a temporary injunction prohibiting the use of the chancery court's order. All obstacles were now thought cleared for the beginning of Little Rock's voluntary integration program on the day after Labor Day, September 2.

Meanwhile, members of the school board heard that Governor Faubus was considering calling out the National Guard to defy the federal court's integration order. Winthrop Rockefeller, appointed by the Governor to head the Arkansas Industrial Development Commission and anxious to entice industry to the state, pleaded with Governor Faubus on Sunday not to take any action that would set back industrial progress for years. Governor Faubus indicated that he had not yet made up his mind but that he greatly feared violence. He apparently made his decision to call out the National Guard on

Monday morning and the proclamation was issued that afternoon.

When Roy Harris heard this news that evening in Georgia,
he later commented, "I sat there . . . just scratching my head
and wondering if he called 'em out *for* us or *agin'* us." Governor Faubus was said to have complained to his friends
that afternoon: "I can't win. . . . If there's trouble or violence
out there tomorrow, the integration crowd will say I provoked it by bringing in troops. But if I don't call the Guard
and some children are killed, the other side will say the
blood is on my hands. I've got to act on the side of safety.
When I testified in chancery court last week, I said there
might be violence. Now, I'm convinced of it." Thus it was
that National Guardsmen and state troopers turned back
nine Negro students who tried to enter Central High School
on September 4, after Judge Davies had directed the school
board to disregard the troops and to permit Negroes to attend
classes at a special hearing on September 3, the first day of
school.

Governor Faubus called out the Guard just a few days
after the first session of the Eighty-Fifth Congress had ended
and I was still in Washington preparing to return home to
spend the fall with my people. While there had been indications that the integration program approved by the courts
would run into some difficulty, it did not seem likely that
such drastic action would be taken to prevent violence. I
arrived in Little Rock on Thursday, September 5, and made
my first public comment that evening. Being relatively unin-
formed on details of the crisis, I had only this to say: "The
whole situation is so new to me it's hard to say anything at
all. I grant he [Faubus] has the duty to maintain law and
order. The first thing we now must do is to try to re-establish
a spirit of calmness so the orderly processes of law can prevail."

That day the school board asked Judge Davies to suspend temporarily the plan for integrating. A hearing was set for Saturday morning. In the meantime, I began to think of ways I could be of assistance. On Friday, I received a call from Bob Estabrook of the *Washington Post* suggesting that I call former President Truman, who was known to be a friend of Governor Faubus, to ask him to appeal to the Governor to withdraw the troops. I was reluctant to make such a request to Mr. Truman and also was not sure of the timing, since the federal court would meet the next morning. Any suspension of the School Board Plan would change the situation somewhat and it seemed best for me to wait for further judicial action. A temporary postponement of integration by court order might be deemed a satisfactory solution to the Governor, who could then disband the National Guard and leave to the federal courts the final decision as to the date for peaceful integration to begin.

With the city tense and expectant, the federal district court convened that Saturday. After a brief hearing, Judge Davies ruled that "this Court is not persuaded that upon the tenuous showing made by the petitions this morning that it should suspend enforcement of the petitioners' plan of integration." The school board then announced that it considered its plan still in effect and that Central High School would "be open Monday for all students."

That Sunday morning, I addressed the congregation of the Second Baptist Church, my home church, reporting to them on my work as head of the Southern Baptist Convention. Then I went back to the Sam Peck Hotel, where I spent the afternoon contemplating this grave challenge to the spiritual strength and social consciousness of Little Rock. I was tormented by the fact that my home city was drifting toward a crisis. A head-on clash between state and federal authority seemed imminent. The lawyers called it a Constitutional

crisis. Nothing was being done to avert it. What is a congressman's responsibility in such a situation? If it were a
flood or tornado, and federal emergency help were required,
the congressman would certainly act. Then should he not
also act in a situation in which the misfortune centered
around human relations rather than physical forces?

I decided to act. I called President Truman, as I had been
requested to do, and he assured me he would do all he could
to help. Governor Faubus was interviewed that evening on
a special television program by a panel of correspondents,
and his moderate presentation of the need to preserve order,
and his denial of opposition to integration, gave me hope that
a quick and peaceful solution would be found. I spoke again
that evening at the Immanuel Baptist Church, already committed to make my good offices available as mediator and
anxious to draw on the spiritual resources of our people to
help remedy the situation.

Monday morning, September 9, I called Presidential Assistant Sherman Adams at the White House to say that, in the
existing difficulties over integration of Little Rock Central
High School, I wanted to be as helpful as possible. I had no
qualms about calling the President's right-hand man because
we had developed a close friendship in Congress ten years
before. "Is there anything I can do?" I asked. He indicated
that there might be and that he appreciated my call very
much. Although nothing definite came out of the conversation, it served as the beginning of the negotiations leading
to the Newport, Rhode Island, meeting. When Sherman
asked for some specific steps that might be taken, I suggested
that the President invite the Governor to Washington for a
conference. Though I had no information whatever on that
point and had not talked to the Governor at all, I was convinced he would accept. Sherman asked some questions about
the Governor—his point of view, his philosophy, and his back-

ground. I explained that in dealing with Governor Faubus he would not be confronting a stubborn, last-ditch segregationist governor, and pointed out that quite aside from the question of the propriety of the Governor's action (I thought he had been wrong in going against the court orders by excluding the Negroes, not in calling out the Guard necessarily), one would have difficulty in proving insincerity. I told Sherman that there was no doubt whatever as to the final outcome—that the federal government would sustain its court orders—but my one great concern was that the Governor not be driven into the arms of the few extremists in the Southern governors' group and that the federal authorities avoid taking such drastic steps as to deprive Arkansas of an opportunity (which still exists) to be a proving ground for moderate alterations in school administration that would eventually comply with the judicial requirements. Sherman was rather sympathetic on this score.

Later in the day I called C. E. Lowry, an insurance executive who had served as the head of the Good Government League, a reform movement which sponsored the successful drive to give Little Rock a city manager form of government. Mr. Lowry thought it was a good idea for me to get in touch with the Governor and he offered his services in arranging a conference. While I considered myself a friend of the Governor, we had followed the traditional Arkansas political pattern of going our separate ways, and we had not had much opportunity to work together on governmental matters. Lowry asked his friend, W. J. Smith, one of the Governor's attorneys, to meet with me at his office. Smith and I lost little time in preliminaries. I asked what he thought the Governor's attitude would be if the President were to invite him. (Sherman had asked me to make inquiries on this point.) Smith said he knew the Governor would accept, then he walked to the phone and put me in touch with the Governor.

I asked, "Would you go?" and he responded, "I don't think I could afford to decline, do you?" I questioned him further, "But, Governor, can I say, 'Yes, you would go'?" And he said, "Yes." I then talked to Sherman again, at length this time. He thought that a favorable answer to three questions should be forthcoming before steps were taken to arrange a conference between the President and the Governor. They were as follows: 1. Would the Governor come with an attitude of constructiveness, with a give-and-take approach, with a desire to achieve something that would preserve the dignity and authority of federal law? 2. Would the Governor indicate that he expected to comply with court orders, that he would avoid defiance, and would accept jurisdiction of federal authority in the field of school integration? 3. Would the Governor indicate that "upon the President's request" he would remove troops from the high school?

Mr. Smith quickly made an engagement for me to see Governor Faubus and drove me from Lowry's office to the Mansion. Within moments I was in the Governor's private quarters where we spent an hour going over the whole situation. His attitude, from my point of view, was very satisfactory. On the first point, there was no doubt about his desire to work constructively with the President and to avoid a showdown that would aggravate the tension. The Governor, of course, gave a qualified answer to points two and three, as I expected him to, but he had enough to say concerning his basic purpose of preserving law and order to make a convincing case for his actions in preventing violence, rather than preventing integration.

At the close of our meeting, the Governor authorized me to say that he would be glad to see the President. (At that stage, no point had been made of the initiation of the request for a conference—whether the President should invite him to Newport or the Governor should request a conference—but

Sherman Adams eventually took the position that the request for a conference should come from the Governor and the Governor agreed to this procedure.) In this initial conference the Governor told me that he was convinced that the overwhelming sentiment of the state and of Little Rock was in opposition to the admission of the nine Negroes to Central High School and to any further steps under the plan approved by the school board and upheld by the federal courts.

As I left the Mansion, the Governor said, "If I go to see the President, I want you and Winthrop Rockefeller to go with me." (That Winthrop did not go can perhaps be attributed to the fact that he was out of the state.) I was excited by the prospect of the conference and was hopeful that it would produce accord. On the basis of public declarations, the two heads of government did not seem to be far apart, and the Governor had said that he would not defy the courts. (Adams was later to ask that the request for a conference make reference to his intentions on this point.)

I departed from Little Rock with my wife later that same afternoon to spend a few days at the home of my father in Russellville, seventy-five miles west of Little Rock. We stopped at the town of Morrilton for dinner and I tried to call the White House. I found the lines busy and was not able to get in touch with Sherman until 11:00 P.M. by his time, after I had reached Russellville. My opening comment, "I'm afraid I got you out of bed," was confirmed, but he apparently was not upset. It was in this conversation that Sherman indicated that the idea of the President's inviting Faubus should give way to a request from the Governor, directed to the President, suggesting that a conference would be helpful. Early in the discussion, he emphasized that all of this was in response to my offer to be helpful and that the White House did not wish to be in an attitude of initiating anything. I gave him all necessary assurances on that point.

I spent Tuesday and Wednesday, September 10 and 11, at my father's home and was in constant telephone contact with the White House and the Governor's Mansion during that time. An enormous amount of time was spent in talking to Little Rock and Washington in negotiating the terms for the Newport meeting. Among other things, the exact language for the telegrams to be exchanged had to be agreed upon. True to their code, the telephone operators handled the calls in routine fashion but let drop indications of interest in the fact that some rather historic calls were coming over the little Russellville switchboard.

On Tuesday I talked at least five times with the White House and about as many times with Governor Faubus. After Sherman indicated that I should help create the wording of the Governor's request for an audience with the President, I gave him some intimation of what the Governor should say and would say, and he commented here and there —reminding me that it was "my responsibility" and "my message" and that these were my overtures. I could understand his reason for being emphatic on that point, but he had some very clear ideas about what the telegram should and should not say. The Governor capitulated on language at practically every point, made a suggestion or two which Sherman said would not alter the administration's approval of the idea in general, and finally it was agreed, when I read the draft of the request to Adams, that it would go in just that form. The Governor said he was satisfied with the wording and I thought everything was in shape, until an hour after the telegram should have been sent. Then I had a call from W. J. Smith saying that we should change the first sentence. Before going into the nature of the change, I protested vigorously, and Bill said, "Okay, the telegram will go through as agreed on." He accepted my explanation that it would mean starting all over again, would undo two days' work, and would put me and the Governor both in an embarrassing position, since I had read the message to the White House and they had said, "If received in that form, the President would certainly grant a conference." I had always regarded myself as serving the Governor's wishes in this matter, even though he and I did not see eye to eye regarding his use of troops, and he had said when I left the Mansion on Monday, "This would be the greatest favor you ever did a governor if you help us work it out."

We reached several delicate points in the various stages of the developments which followed. In the first instance, my ability to carry out my role in the early negotiations depended on my success in keeping out of the newspapers. The *Washington Post*, however, learned of what was taking place and let it leak out that they knew someone had been in touch with Sherman Adams—and he naturally did not like it one bit. He did not blame me, but he said that, if such leaks were repeated, obviously he could not go on with the step-by-step discussion of arrangements for a conference. I think I satisfied him that such minor breaks are inevitable. The reporters saw me go into the Mansion, and they could not help speculating on the significance of this, coupling it with the fact that Sherman and I had been friends for a long time.

Another serious question concerned whether the Governor would accept a federal court summons for a hearing scheduled on September 20 on a petition for a preliminary injunction against his and the Arkansas National Guard's obstructing integration. His acceptance of this summons on Tuesday relieved much of this tension and made my work more manageable. With Faubus expressing respect for the orderly processes of law, the administration was more likely to be willing to negotiate. The next problem to arise concerned the wording of the telegram to be sent to the President. As agreed upon, it read, "I have accepted summons of the U.S. District

Court, etc.," but the Governor's lawyer wanted it to read, "I have been *served* with summons." After it was made clear that I had given Sherman firm assurance, on Governor Faubus' authority, that the telegram in that exact form would be sent, he withdrew his objections. It seemed a very minor point to me, since the Governor did actually accept the summons.

On Wednesday, Sherman and I talked a little about the basis for a discussion, while we worked out final details of the message exchange. We needed to have some clear idea of the use of military force by the Governor, when it should cease, and how it could be used to enforce the court orders, not to obstruct those orders. While I was unable to clarify any of these points, I could say that Faubus was prepared to go along fully and was eager to get the meeting behind us. After several talks during the day, Adams said to me, "You have rendered a great public service and I have only praise for your work."

All along in these telephone conversations, however, I was conscious of not being in the circle of political advisors for either of the principals. This was not really a handicap. The only stage in the proceedings at which I had reason to feel that advisors were unduly hampering steps for the conference was at the time of sending the telegram. It was therefore a source of great personal satisfaction to help bridge the gap between the federal and state governments. It was good that there was only one occasion on which anyone other than the Governor himself was a party to negotiations at the Little Rock end of the line. It was at this stage that I gave Sherman the Governor's private unlisted telephone number since I feared there might be a mishap resulting from the indirect conversations.

When Governor Faubus agreed to indicate his respect for the courts in his message to the President, I felt we had the basis for a productive conference. The Governor seemed anxious for a truce, such as integration's beginning by mid-term after the situation had settled down. He also seemed to think that the method of integration, starting at the high-school level, was not the most suitable and suggested that the plan be changed, permitting integration to begin at the first grade. He had a strong desire for conciliation but sought time to soften the adjustment. It seemed ironic that the federal courts were forcing a show-down that neither side wanted, when true "justice" might best have been served by traditional judicial calm and exhaustive deliberation. Governor Faubus also complained of the lack of advance support from the leading fifty businessmen in Little Rock, of what he called the "country-club" set, when he appealed to them on behalf of community support for enforcing moderate integration under the Court decree. That he was making concessions to the lawful processes of government was shown by his rejecting the idea of calling a conference of Southern governors to support his present stand.

Sherman Adams took a dim view of the Governor's idea that, if an official or unofficial truce could be arranged, lasting from the opening of the schools to mid-term, integration as originally planned by the school board, or revised along lines he suggested, could then begin. Regardless of this, Sherman was anxious to help the Governor find a solution which would meet the needs of the people of Arkansas and still conform with the law of the land.

My own view is stated in my diary citation of Wednesday, September 11:

It seems to me that time, not substance, presents the difficulty. The Governor is not opposed to the School Board decision being carried out, he simply thinks that a delay is essential to the maintenance of peace. If the conference does not produce some kind of accord, it will be because the Justice Department and the

Governor are too far apart on this point. I told Sherman that I felt sure the Justice Department should be told by him that some flexibility must come into the discussions, that the Supreme Court decision was startling in its newness albeit the old order simply did not suffice, and that they should not object to the staffing of the U.S. Marshal's office to supplement the State Police—or, if confined to local authorities, the city police and the county sheriff's deputies.

The Justice Department would not be happy over the concessions as to time that the President might make, but I am hopeful that he will be convinced from the Governor's presentation that some delay would be exceedingly helpful. We need a breather. I think I influenced Sherman on the question of help from the Federal Government to protect the students and maintain order. At any rate, he said that while the Government would have to insist that the maintenance of order is the State's responsibility, Federal help would be available on the Governor's request.

It was at 12:15 P.M. Wednesday that the Governor's telegram was sent by W. J. Smith to Newport.

At 2:30 Sherman called to read me the President's answer. He told me to release it in fifteen minutes. I read it to the Governor and he said he would call the newspapers at once. I relaxed. My own participation in the pre-Newport talks was finally made known, after much newspaper speculation, by Presidential Press Secretary Jim Hagerty, when he answered a question about it on that Wednesday's news conference releasing the President's and the Governor's telegrams.

This was the Governor's message to the President:

Dear Mr. President. I have accepted summons from the United States District Court, Eastern District of Arkansas, to appear before that Court on September 20th to answer certain allegations in litigation affecting the high school in Little Rock. Recognizing that we jointly share great responsibility under the Federal Constitution, I feel that it is advisable for us to counsel together in determining my course of action as Chief Executive of the State of Arkansas with reference to the responsibility placed upon me by the State and Federal Constitutions.

The United States District Court has already entered an order relative to the integration of the high school in Little Rock, and this order has been affirmed by the Circuit Court of Appeals.

All good citizens must of course obey all proper orders of our Courts and it is certainly my desire to comply with the order that has been issued by the District Court in this case, consistent with my responsibility under the Constitution of the United States and that of Arkansas.

May I confer with you on this matter at your earliest convenience.

The President's answer:

I have your telegram in which you request a meeting with me. Would it suit your convenience to come to my office on Naval Base, Newport, either Friday, September 13, at 3:00 PM or Saturday AM, 14th, at 9 o'clock. If you would let my office know your method of transportation to the Newport area my staff will arrange to have you met and brought to the Base.

(signed) Dwight D. Eisenhower

When I returned to Little Rock from Russellville on Thursday, the reporters literally besieged me. The newsmen and photographers found me in a suburban cafeteria and they completely disrupted an informal gathering of my staff and family around the luncheon table. I could not complain about it. Things had begun to pop and I had learned enough of the problems of newspaper and radio men to sympathize with them. I finally confirmed the reports of my projected trip to Newport with the Governor at his request. I had cancelled a speaking engagement in San Antonio, Texas, which had, of course, tipped off the press concerning my change in plans. The announcement of my role as mediator was the signal for representatives of all media of mass communication to descend upon me, and it was not for several weeks that I was able to have any privacy, while world attention focused on Little Rock.

The Governor, his private secretary, Arnold Sikes, two pilots, and I left Little Rock early Friday morning in a chartered plane for the conference which had been scheduled for Saturday morning. We encountered a thunderstorm which tossed us about but the Governor was tranquil. He actually slept through some of it. We stopped for lunch and refueling at Roanoke, Virginia. The Governor and I walked into the lunchroom unnoticed. On the front page of the newspapers, which seemed to stare at us from the newsstand, was a two-column picture of me, but no one seemed to recognize us. The anonymity was rather welcome after the preceding hectic day. Adams had arranged for us to be met at the Providence Airport by an aide and escorted to a hotel. The character of the reception given us at the Rhode Island airport convinced me that sentiment in that area was not friendly and it became obvious within a short time that this reflected national sentiment (outside the deep South). No one representing the Governor of Rhode Island or the Mayor of Providence was on hand to welcome us. There were curious crowds but no cheering. It was rather pathetic to see Governor Faubus looking vainly for some sign of enthusiasm. I was beginning by that time to understand the criticisms of the President's decision to confer with the Governor and to realize that I was becoming a target for attack by extremists on both sides for my efforts to compose differences.

However, two telegrams provided one humorous reflection of the problems we faced. The one to Faubus was from a man in Florida and ran about as follows: "Pay no attention to that fellow traveling with you. Hays is an integrationist and should be repudiated." The Governor smiled and handed it to me. A few minutes later, I received a telegram from a

Virginian which had this to say in substance: "Southerners should be ashamed of your Governor. Hope you can supply some sense for the Newport Conference." I could not resist showing this one to Faubus with the comment that we were even now. The only trouble was that we had the responsibility for developing a course of action that would be satisfactory to the federal and state governments and still please people of the opinions reflected in these messages. It was a large order and we did not deceive ourselves about the size of the task. I was confident, however, that the Governor was anxious to cooperate fully.

The Governor, Sikes, and I ate dinner in the hotel suite. The management and city police cooperated in giving us privacy. Newsmen were swarming all over the hotel and except for police protection we would doubtless have gotten little sleep that night. We were up early Saturday morning and, after an escorted drive to the airport, we boarded a helicopter provided by the White House for the short flight to Newport. There we were met by Sherman Adams himself and other White House aides and were whisked through the battery of television cameras, radio reporters, and newsmen, to which I had become accustomed, to the President's office. The President shook hands with his usual cordiality. "How are you, Brooks?" he asked, and it was easy for me to say I felt fine. At that moment I did. Sherman suggested that it might be helpful for "them" to have a talk by themselves. While the President and the Governor talked, Sherman and I sat in the reception room discussing the problem and when the two chiefs walked out we were ready with some ideas as to the direction in which the conversation should move.

President Eisenhower and Governor Faubus were in the President's private office only about fifteen minutes, less time than Sherman had thought they might wish to have alone. The President (in sport coat and blue shirt, looking in the pink) came out with the Governor and suggested, as he helped Sherman rearrange the chairs, "Let's just sit here and talk." That we did for nearly two hours. The atmosphere was fairly relaxed. The Governor, being closer to the problem, was a bit solemn, and the President at that stage doubtless did not foresee the dilemma that would confront him within ten days. Before the meeting ended, the President suggested that Attorney General Brownell should join us. He and Jim Hagerty came in for the last part of the discussion.

My position was rather unusual. I was there "by invitation" of Governor Faubus, and, since Adams had indicated approval of my coming, it might be added "by invitation" of the President. Months later, Adams remarked, when I said that it might be well for history's sake to record some of the talk, that the conversation was subject to the customary restrictions on executive communications and that (speaking to me) "You were invited by the President and would be bound by the usual rules." I thought so, too. But at the same time he was advised of my desire to reveal these few details and offered no objection.

At Newport, Governor Faubus, in his usual unhurried way, stressed the importance of the time element—a way should be found, he felt, to get federal court "relief" for Little Rock until the Supreme Court had ruled on the validity of the state Constitutional amendments and statutes ("interposition" and several other measures) approved either by the people of Arkansas in the 1956 election or the Arkansas General Assembly in 1957. The President conceded that time was a factor but thought that the matter fell so completely within the jurisdiction of the courts that little could be done by the Executive in that regard. There was some discussion of the various ways of complying with the Supreme Court decision, and the Governor expressed the view that the plan advanced by Superintendent Virgil Blossom and his school board, and later approved by the courts, was subject to criticism. The President was inclined to think that any advantage in other plans, such as beginning in the first grade instead of the twelfth, would be offset by disadvantages. Differences between Louisville and Little Rock were discussed briefly. I remember how emphatic the President was in assuring the Governor that he regards the states as responsible for maintaining law and order and that the Governor's primary responsibility should be respected. "I do not criticize you for calling out the Guard—our only difference is that I would have given them different instructions."

The Governor at one stage said, "I expect to send the Guard home." (This he did on September 20.)

The political aspects of the problem were touched upon, and the President expressed sympathy for those of us who live so close to the problem, at the same time minimizing the seriousness of the so-called political revolt.

The statements issued in the afternoon covered the substance of the rest of the conference.

I had the feeling when the meeting ended that we were leaving loose ends, and wish now that an afternoon session had been set up. There was unfinished business. Still I can see why the President would think that the matter had been sufficiently explored and that the conclusions, which were later in the day put in writing, were sufficient. My doubts about the adequacy of these conclusions were based on the desire to see a carefully drawn up agreement approved by all parties. I had come to Newport confident that such an agreement could be reached, and both the President and Governor Faubus acted in a manner that strengthened that opinion. What made me uneasy, however, was the uncertainty about the "time element" that both sides agreed was the key to a final solution. The rigidity of Brownell's position on this factor gave me some forebodings, but I was still hopeful of working out a timetable with the Governor when we returned to Little Rock. It is obvious to me now that this step should have been taken at Newport, where the conditions for a settlement were generally favorable.

We were about to say good-bye when Sherman asked me to tell the President about "the Alabama horse deal," a story Congressman Grant had related. Here it is: A farmer approached his neighbor and asked: "How much do you want for that horse?" "$100." "Sold." And he laid out the cash. After the buyer left he thought: "That fella wanted the horse mighty bad—didn't argue about the price—just grabbed it up—must know more about the horse than I do." So he went over to his friend and repurchased him for $150. Then the other one thought: "He wanted that horse back pretty bad—must be a better horse than I thought." So he went back around to buy him for $200. So it went till they had the *bid* up to $1,500 when a dealer from another county came in and paid $2,000 for the animal. When he heard about it, the original owner went over to his friend's house and confirmed it—"Well, what did you do that for—*we were both making a good living off of him.*" I added, "That's the way some people think we operate government finances." This was the only light touch of the meeting.

We agreed that the horde of newsmen outside were entitled to some information on conference results and that Hagerty should promise them a statement later.

When we got back to the hotel in Providence, not much time was left for preparing the release which we had promised for two o'clock. But the Governor was apparently wrapped in thought. Finally, I asked if he would like for me to draft something for him to look at and he said, "I wish you would." I quickly wrote out the substance of the Governor's position as outlined to the President that morning. He made only a minor change. "That's all right," he said, so I called Newport and read it to Adams. He read the text of what the President would say and I relayed it to the Governor. I believe both he and Adams made minor suggestions for change which were quickly agreed to. Here are the statements:

STATEMENT BY GOVERNOR FAUBUS

The President and I have had a friendly and constructive discussion of the problem of compliance with court orders respecting the high schools of Little Rock. This trip to Newport has been worthwhile from my point of view. I recognize that the situation called for clarification and I assured the President of my desire to cooperate with him in carrying out the duties resting upon both of us under the Federal Constitution. In addition I must harmonize my actions under the Federal Constitution with the requirements of the Constitution of Arkansas.

I have never expressed any personal opinion regarding the Supreme Court decision of 1954 which ordered integration. That is not relevant. That decision is the law of the land and must be obeyed.

At the same time, it is evident even from the language of the decision itself that changes necessitated by Court orders cannot be accomplished overnight.

The people of Little Rock are law abiding and I know that they expect to obey valid court orders. In this they shall have my support. In so doing it is my responsibility to protect the people from violence in any form.

As I interpret the President's public statement, the national administration has no thought of challenging this fact. In meeting this obligation, it is essential in proceeding to implement the orders of the court that the complexities of integration be patiently understood by all those in federal authority as well as others.

When I assure the President, as I have already done, that I ex-

pect to accept the decisions of the court, I entertain the hope that
the Department of Justice and the federal judiciary will act with
understanding and patience in discharging their duties.

STATEMENT BY PRESIDENT EISENHOWER

At the request of Governor Faubus of Arkansas I met with him
this morning in a constructive discussion regarding the carrying
out of the order of the Federal Court in the matter of the high
schools of Little Rock.

The Governor stated his intention to respect the decisions of
the United States District Court and to give his full cooperation
in carrying out his responsibilities in respect to these decisions.
In doing so, I recognize the inescapable responsibility resting
upon the Governor to preserve law and order in his state. I am
gratified by his constructive and cooperative attitude at our
meeting.

I have assured the governor of the cooperation of federal officials. I was pleased to hear from the governor of this progress
already made in the elimination of segregation in other activities
in the state of Arkansas.

I am sure it is the desire of the governor not only to observe the
supreme law of the land but to use the influence of his office in
orderly progress of the plans which are already the subject of the
order of the Court.

I attribute the Governor's pensiveness that day to the fact
that Brownell seemed to have blocked a definite commitment
to work for delays in further court action, thus permitting
a court determination of the validity of state statutes on interposition and the sovereignty commission. What courses of
action would then be available would be clarified by such
court rulings. If the state laws were upheld, the situation
would be eased, because then the Governor could say, "I
am following state law." If they were invalidated, then he
would have an answer to the cry that one heard in parts of
Arkansas, "You are under a mandate of the people to prevent

any degree of integration." My assumption is based not so much on what was said at Newport but what was *not* said. The Governor held a press conference before we left, handling himself very well, I thought, particularly when unfriendly questioning took place.

I left the party at LaGuardia and took a night plane for Fort Worth. We encountered severe weather which made it difficult to sleep, and at Dallas, radio and newspaper men met me at 3 A.M. They asked for a radio interview. "At this hour?" I exclaimed. "Couldn't turn us down, could you? We've waited two hours for your late plane." I tried to comply but was too exhausted to present an intelligible statement after only two hours sleep. That Sunday I spoke three times in Fort Worth to large crowds.

In the afternoon I called the Governor, who was now back in Little Rock. In the middle of the conversation he asked, "Where are you?" When I told him I was in Fort Worth and was going on to Oklahoma City for several days, he said, "I'd appreciate your coming back to Little Rock for a day or two if you can." I agreed at once, fearing that something had gone wrong. I was confident that the Governor did not want a showdown with the federal government, but I had sensed the fact that terrific new pressures were being applied and that he was in a difficult situation. Indeed, the visit of Governor Griffin of Georgia to Little Rock in August had greatly encouraged local extremists and had exacerbated the problem considerably from the standpoint of spreading fear of violence.

I am often asked if I think violence would have taken place had the Governor not predicted stoutly in state court on Thursday before the school opening that it *would* take place and shortly thereafter placed the troops at Central High School. My own opinion is that probably it would not have taken place, but one can only speculate. It has always been my opinion, however, that the Governor was sincere in his fear of the outbreak of violence. He very likely considered his actions quite similar to those of Governor Shivers of Texas who called out the Texas Rangers to stop integration in Mansfield. He probably overlooked the differences in the two situations, such as the absence of a court-approved plan in Mansfield and the contrasting kinds of Negro populations. What he could have been hoping for was an agreement to suspend steps to begin the school board's program and an understanding that this move was initiated solely to preserve peace and order.

Undoubtedly it became evident that a majority of Little Rock people were opposed to desegregation even when the solid Negro opinion to the contrary is taken into account. In the final analysis it was this sentiment rather than the threat of violence that accounted for most of the Governor's actions. When, eventually, on September 20, he sent the troops home in compliance with the court order, he pointed to his effort to live up to his Newport commitment and defended his action in calling out the Guard in the first place to "keep the peace." There is some logic to the argument that *temporarily* (but only temporarily and very briefly) he could order the Negroes to be excluded without defying the federal government. At times, during all of these rapidly shifting situations, I wished the Governor were a lawyer. I saw so clearly the necessity of compliance with valid court orders, by changing the Guard instructions or substituting state police, that I persisted in efforts to interpret the problem to him in terms that would fit into his own moderate views of state sovereignty.

But he had too few political advisors who sympathized with those moderate views. Some of them exploited fully his promise not to force integration upon an "unwilling" community. Some of these advisors were from eastern Arkansas where it must be conceded that there is a complex and delicate race problem. I was handicapped greatly by not being able to confront those who were, in my absence, cancelling my arguments. The Governor had been impressed by my reasoning that federal law would ultimately prevail. Then in came the "practical men." "Don't let Brooks talk you into something, he's too visionary," I could hear them say. And the Governor, priding himself on political acumen, accepted this reasoning. He gave me every chance, however, to present my case. Never at any point did he show impatience, nor did he seem to tire of efforts to find a way out. He was not happy with the turn of events, and I do not believe he is happy about it today. There were moments of exaltation, perhaps, when the glow of acclaim in the deep South brought a smile to the countenance that had come to symbolize the region's resistance, but underneath was a wistfulness for a smoother path to political glory and power.

I became very fond of the Governor during our long vigils at the Mansion. He called me his bishop (he is a Baptist) and I know he gave ear when I tried to picture the grandeur of the other course of defiance—defiance of the interpositionists (or nullificationists to be more accurate).

I was pretty sure at one stage that I had convinced him that a change of orders for the Guard would be entirely consistent with his promise not to force desegregation on an unwilling community. The courts were the ones doing the forcing. He would merely preserve order. If Negroes were excluded he would be guilty of military enforcement of segregation and he would have no judicial support for that position.

He was, I argued, in danger of adopting the philosophy of Jim Johnson, his 1956 opponent, whose extremism had led to his defeat. With regard to the will of the people, I cautioned the Governor that the popular Jeffersonian idea of local determination could not withstand the power of a federal court order based not on a division of powers in school administration but on the Bill of Rights. It makes a difference when a principle, as enunciated in the Supreme Court decision of 1954 for general acceptance, has been frozen into specific application by federal judges as in the Little Rock case. Moreover, the Jeffersonian argument is really in the other direction. The weakness in the pattern of the extremists' opposition is that while condemning the federal government for dictating to the states, they are dictating to the communities by denying a local district's right to desegregate. Local autonomy in school matters has generally been a cherished Jeffersonian principle and it may yet be the key to the solution of this problem (though I would not contend that a district should be permitted to do anything it wished, wholly unrestricted by basic Constitutional principles, either state and federal).

I pointed out to the Governor that he should not depend on his private polls showing a stronger local sentiment against admission of the nine Negro students, but rather on the official action of Little Rock's duly elected school board (some chosen over segregationist opposition). The Jeffersonian principle of local control surely contemplates respect for the judgments of the people's locally elected officials.

Applying this to the Little Rock situation, I am confident that while a majority would prefer the segregated schools, even a larger majority would sustain the duly elected school board in compliance policies and would oppose militarily enforced segregation as well as militarily enforced integration.

During this time, some of my most agonizing moments were when the newsmen met me at the Mansion gates, eager for news, and there was no news. I sympathized with them and began to develop an eagerness myself to have big news.

It would be the conquest of the forces of unceasing resistance and sectional strife. The rule of law would have a significant triumph. (That day will yet come. I hope the newsmen who despaired with me will still be around.)

Governor Faubus and I held numerous conversations at the Mansion between Monday, September 16, and Friday morning, September 20, when the federal court met to consider the school situation. I kept urging the Governor that he recognize the fact that the power of the federal government would, in one way or another, be used to uphold the dignity and authority of its courts. At this stage, the Governor need only have instructed the Guard to admit rather than exclude the Negro students. The ideal arrangement under which our dual system of state and federal sovereignties is maintained could thus again prove its resiliency. He would still have been free from the baseless charges of this 1956 extremist opposition that he, the Governor, would be responsible for integration. (It is rather fanciful to call Little Rock's plan "integration"—it is, to be sure, compliance with the 1954 decision but would more properly be considered "desegregation," and there is a difference. As I have pointed out before, the Supreme Court really did not require integration. The Little Rock plan, if fully completed, would never raise the ratio of Negro students to more than 5 per cent of the total in the "integrated" schools.)

On Monday, the Governor indicated his willingness to send the National Guard home provided that the target date for admission of Negro students was changed to a later date, possibly as early as September 30. He was quite concerned, however, that the constitutionality of the Arkansas sovereignty laws be determined as soon as possible, so he would not be caught between conflicting directives concerning his lawful actions. By negotiation with various prominent people in both public and private life, I arrived at this proposed

course of action for the Governor: (1) that he write a letter
to the parents of the Negro children asking them voluntarily
to keep their children out of school until a set date arrived
(we had assurances they would agree); (2) that he guarantee
to use his influence to create a peaceful atmosphere; (3) that
he see that the local school authorities provide private tutors
for the nine Negro children during the interim period; and
(4) that he pledge to use his office to insure the peace after
the given deadline for admission. One of the major stumbling
blocks was the attitude of the Justice Department, which
would make no commitment not to take Faubus to court.
While this department was also determined not to wait for
state court action on the sovereignty laws, it did indicate that
federal action might be withdrawn once the school was integrated. The Governor would not write such a letter under
those conditions. He seemed willing to go along with Sherman Adams in the use of state patrols to control the school
situation once the National Guard was withdrawn, but he
was impatient with Attorney General Brownell for not meeting his legal responsibilities. He was even willing to make a
public declaration defending President Eisenhower from
attacks by members of the Democratic party who wanted
immediate action by the administration, but he feared that
such a statement would hurt the President in identifying him
with the segregationists.

I was then faced with a situation in which there was a
possibility of bringing Governor Faubus and Sherman Adams
together, but Herbert Brownell seemed determined on a
judicial showdown. I also knew that the President would
listen to Adams' counsel of moderation as long as there was a
chance for conciliation but that, if that chance appeared to
be fading, the counsel of Brownell, who apparently favored
ultimate extreme federal action, would gain the upper hand.
This impasse extended into Tuesday when both sides began

to weary of the exchange and become somewhat belligerent. Adams was rather abrupt on the phone and said that the Governor could do anything he wanted to, if he had no regard for the consequences. Meanwhile, for the first time, I saw evidence of the influence of extremists on Faubus, who now told me that he could not let the federal government ram integration down the throat of the city. He was still considering the removal of the troops, however, coupled with the issuance of a statement "guaranteeing" to preserve order. This action was, of course, based on the assumption that there be at least a temporary stay of the court injunction. It seemed to me, however, that the Governor now occupied two irreconcilable positions—one, that he respected the courts and federal law, and, two, that he was not willing to "inte- grate" an unwilling city.

Since Governor Faubus was still considering removal of the National Guard before the court hearing of Friday, Sep- tember 20, many other questions arose. Thurgood Marshall of the NAACP, who was in town, gave private assurance to sources available to me that the Negro students would stay out of school for two weeks, provided this time be used to assure compliance with the court order rather than serve to enable agitators to stir up trouble. This raised the question of how much violence might occur at this stage if the Guard were removed. Could the city police handle the situation? FBI Chief J. Edgar Hoover was reluctant to have his investi- gating forces now present in Little Rock used for policing purposes. Various other alternatives, such as having the number of deputies available to the federal marshal in- creased, were considered. The general attitude became once again deep concern over an open split between the state and federal governments.

Meanwhile, Washington sources informed me that the Justice Department was not eager for a fight and was deeply alarmed at the possibility of a showdown of force against force. Another alternative became available for the Governor in helping him resolve his dilemma. If the National Guard were federalized, then integration could be enforced without his open advocacy. All that would be required of the Governor then would be for him to plead for peaceful acceptance of this move, not to object to the federalizing, with his obvious explanation to the segregationists being that he no longer had any control over the situation.

In the discussions I had with Sherman Adams early Wednesday morning he indicated that he was not anxious to have the Governor enjoined from blocking integration, but that he was also not convinced that federalizing the Guard was the answer. When I visited the Mansion that afternoon, Governor Faubus looked as if he were prepared for litigation and ready for a fight. I was not too concerned over the possibility of his being enjoined on Friday, because this might be a means for him to "save face," but his growing irritation made the possibilities of a peaceful adjustment appear remote. Meanwhile, Mayor Mann called, imploring that I help him get advance notice of the withdrawal of the Guard, so his police would be alerted to prevent violence. Shortly thereafter, Harry Ashmore, executive editor of *The Arkansas Gazette*, called to tell me that he thought Adams' approach was wrong and that he felt the time had come for me to pull out of the negotiations, since apparently the whole matter would have to be settled in court.

On Wednesday night I decided that the talk with the Governor I had scheduled for Thursday morning was not likely to be productive, so I prepared a short statement primarily to preserve my own position and avoid further involvement, intending to hand it to the reporters at the Mansion gate as I came out. I advised the press that an important statement would be made. However, I talked with Adams early the next morning and he said: "I don't believe I'd do that," and I did not. I was never quite able to relieve the reporters' curiosity concerning the reasons for this action. Adams' request was further proof that the White House was not welcoming a showdown and that they wanted my contact preserved, fragile though it was. The evening on which I promised a statement would be forthcoming "next morning" (the one that never came because Sherman Adams asked me to hold on a little longer), one newsman spoke up: "Mr. Hays, you have been putting out statements that haven't had any meaning—will this one have any meaning?" I flared up a little at that. "I have put out no statements at all—I have only answered questions. You are unkind to say that," I said very crisply. Then I added, "I'm sorry. I'm tired." He held out his hand. "I apologize," he said, "I'm tired, too." I shook hands with him. "It's one o'clock. Let's go to bed," I added.

Here is the statement I had prepared for the reporters:

The time has come for me to give you a brief report on my activities of the last few days, and to say that I will not likely see the Governor again at least until the District Court hearings are completed.

My role has been difficult to describe. It was self-initiated, but both the President and the Governor have made it easy for me to transmit information and suggestions that I thought might be helpful. I am grateful for their confidence.

My conferences with the Governor have been for the purpose of examining all possible alternatives for action by Federal and State authorities including the one being chosen by the Governor to proceed through the Courts. His decision certainly should not be construed as a repudiation of these talks. There have been differences between us, of course, but both of us have had in mind discovery of appropriate methods for achieving the rule of law.

It is my own feeling that ultimately the Supreme Court school decisions of 1954, as interpreted and approved by the Little Rock School Board and the Circuit Court of Appeals, will be upheld and that the Negro students will be peacefully enrolled and instructed under that plan. That is what the rule of law means—it does not mean that only popular laws are to be enforced. Furthermore, it does not mean that we must accept the ruling of the Supreme Court as ultimate wisdom, but it does mean that compliance with that Court's ruling is the only proper course available to us if Constitutional Government is to survive. This poses a hard problem for our city, but I know that regardless of objections to the Court orders the people of our community will abide by them.

I fervently hope that our experience here will be helpful to other areas. The principal factors are popular devotion to law and order and the flexibility of Federal law which should not be imposed by sudden edict. Neither statutory nor decision law can have life without the common consent that time alone can supply.

Late Thursday night my wife and I left for Oklahoma City for the concluding session of the South-wide meeting of the Baptist Brotherhood. From the Biltmore Hotel in that city I called the White House to say to Sherman Adams that I had not had the door slammed on me at the Governor's Mansion, that I was still anxious for my city to be spared the impending disaster. I told him of engagements I had in Kansas City on Saturday and Sunday. He asked if I could cancel them and return to Little Rock. He wanted to continue to use my contact there. He had no other way at that moment of knowing fully the state and local developments. I agreed, of course. It necessitated telephoning Mr. Truman to explain why I would not be at the dinner planned for us by Mayor Bartle and my friend, Joe Culpepper, a Kansas City businessman. "That's all right," Mr. Truman said, and he added, "Brooks, I've been thinking of you and feeling for you." "Thank you, Mr. President," I answered, "but you stood eight years of it; I can stand eight weeks of it." "No," he said, "it's harder on you than on me—I can cuss and you can't!"

In one of several phone conversations I had with Little Rock people during the twenty-four hours I was in Oklahoma City, I learned from Chief of Police Marvin Potts just what his intentions were if Negro students should appear at the high school. He made a clear commitment to use the full police force in an effort to prevent violence. He knew it would be difficult and recognized the gravity of the situation, but he felt sure of his men and he would certainly not show any weakness himself. I knew that he was planning to resign and that he would be happier if he were able to make an honorable exit before the crisis arose, but he did not propose to fade into retirement with even the faintest stain on his record.

There were equivalent promises from his assistant chief, Eugene Smith, another competent peace officer who has since succeeded Mr. Potts.

On Friday, Federal Judge Davies ordered the Governor to end his opposition to judicial authority and directed him to stop interfering with integration at Little Rock Central High School. The following is a summary of the court decision.

THE COURT: It is very clear to this Court from the evidence and the testimony adduced upon the hearing today that the plan of integration adopted by the Little Rock School Board and approved by this Court and the Court of Appeals for the Eighth Circuit has been thwarted by the Governor of Arkansas by the use of National Guard troops. It is equally demonstrable from the testimony here today that there would have been no violence in carrying out the plan of integration, and that there has been no violence.

The petition of the United States of America as amicus curiae for a preliminary injunction against Governor Faubus, General Clinger and Colonel Johnson and all others named in the petition is granted and such injunction shall issue without delay enjoining those respondents from obstructing or preventing by use of the National Guard or otherwise the attendance of Negro students at Little Rock High School under the plan of integration approved by this Court and from otherwise obstructing or interfering with orders of this Court in connection with the plan of integration.

Governor Faubus' attorneys walked out of the courtroom in the middle of the hearing rather than stay to cross-examine witnesses and hear the verdict, thus challenging the court's authority. Three hours after the decision, Governor Faubus went on television to announce his withdrawal of the Guard, in compliance with the order, but he had earlier indicated he would appeal the decision of Judge Davies on the ground that the district court did not have jurisdiction against him. He said that the right of Negro children to attend white schools had been upheld by the Supreme Court but that he hoped "by their own volition the Negroes would refrain from seizing upon that right until such time as there is assurance that it can be accomplished in a peaceful manner." He closed with an appeal for "reason and clear thinking and good order." In Washington, President Eisenhower called the withdrawal of the Guard "a necessary step in the right direction." He went on to say that he was confident that the citizens of Little Rock would demonstrate that in their city proper orders of a United States court would be executed promptly and without disorder.

My wife and I boarded the train for Little Rock early Saturday morning in a driving rain which continued all day. It fitted my mood. Late in the afternoon I was met at a station two hours out of Little Rock by my friend, Clyde Lowry, who drove me the remaining distance in his car so he could counsel with me on the gravity of the situation. My wife continued on the train. Clyde was interested in the political phases of the conflict. He felt that my efforts toward mediation had been applauded but that, since they had apparently failed, I should not jeopardize my political future. It was not the counsel of timidity or defeatism but the product of his deep concern for my political influence and position. Neither of us could see any avenues of further service opening for me. As I look back on it now (and I am sure he would share this feeling), I wonder why we thought that there was nothing left to do.

Back in the familiar surroundings of the Sam Peck Hotel, I could only hope that as the collision between state and federal authorities approached, violence would be avoided and no undue strain placed upon existing relationships. I saw this conflict in the framework of a seething South and a disquieted nation. There were vast repercussions abroad, and I was eager for our national prestige not to be damaged. World peril was too great to permit indifference to the foreign policy aspects of the struggle. I had endeavored in my talks with the Governor to suggest a condition that would not make federal military policing inevitable. An unexpected call from Mayor Mann came early Sunday morning. The Mayor was once again responsible for preserving order in the city and members of the Little Rock police force took over the guard duty as the National Guardsmen left the school. In a public statement, Mr. Mann had urged Little Rock residents to accept integration peacefully and warned that local law enforcement officers would be on hand to deal with persons who did not cooperate. Privately, he now expressed concern to me over the danger that the disorder might be too great to be controlled by his small police force, and he asked for my assistance.

When I had decided to return to Little Rock I told the press that I now considered my responsibilities heavier than ever, since they were related to the preservation of the peace, and I now assured the Mayor of my support. The White House informed me that they wanted to keep the federal government from coming into the picture and hoped that local forces could do the job. The school board met in emergency sessions over the week end but no final decisions were made until Sunday concerning entry of the Negro students on Monday, September 23. It was suggested that the city might need federal financial help, at least, in order to pay for temporary police that might be necessary. Police Chief Potts said again he would do his duty, that he would "defend" all students, white or black, but he balked at pledging an "escort." At this time Sherman Adams indicated that, if requested by appropriate authority, the administration might make troops available at the state border in the event that the situation got out of hand.

Meanwhile, Governor Faubus flew to Georgia to attend the Southern Governors' Conference and left Lieutenant Governor Nathan Gordon as the state's acting chief executive. When asked in Atlanta if he thought the Little Rock police could handle the situation, the Governor replied: "I wouldn't want to say. I don't want to say anything which might tend to be construed to be inflammatory." When asked if he believed there would be violence at the school, however, he answered, "I think so."

Henry Woods, law partner of former Governor Sid Mc-Math, called me on Sunday to say that the Mayor wanted my advice in regard to his effort to maintain order at Central High the next morning—assuming that the Negro students would try to enroll. Would I please come back out to Woods's home for a conference? I was not sure I should go. It might draw me into the orbit of political opposition to Governor Faubus, and I was trying hard to escape involvement in the feud which had developed between McMath and the Governor. McMath and the Mayor were apparently collaborating in plans that at least appeared to the public to have political overtones.

I asked Virgil Blossom what to do. "You should see the Mayor," he said, and he agreed to go with me. His advice was based on the realization that, with the National Guard withdrawn, if violence threatened the next day, any hope of preserving peace would depend upon local police and such other help as the Mayor could muster.

Still we were eager not to be publicly identified with political interests, so we made no public announcement of our destination when we left the hotel.

When we entered the living room of the Woods's home, we found, in addition to Woods and the Mayor, Governor McMath, Ed Dunaway, McMath's close friend and Winthrop Rockefeller's attorney, and Harry Ashmore. The purpose of their conferring, it developed, was to make plans for protecting the Negro students should they appear at the school. No one seemed to know what their intentions were. I was determined not to make any contacts with the NAACP officials, either national or local. I disagreed with their tactics and, in the Little Rock situation, I could not even discuss the question with them without appearing to approve projection of the national organization into Little Rock's difficulties. I knew only one NAACP official and I had assumed that he had had nothing to do with NAACP's pressures on the school board. This official was their lobbyist, Clarence Mitchell, whose attitudes and actions had always appeared, in the few contacts I had had with him, to be honorable. One can oppose, as I do, the national organization's strategy and still believe strongly in their right to function as an agent of their people's interests, just as I believe that White Citizens Councils should not be prevented by court procedures or otherwise from holding meetings or propagating their views. The risks of our governmental system include freedom for organizations to function, even when their methods and objectives are distasteful. These organizations are creatures of freedom.

In the meeting at the Woods residence I do not recall that Governor Faubus was mentioned. It was assumed that the obligation for policing rested on Mayor Mann. I was asked about the White House or Justice Department plans for supplementing local police facilities, but I could bring very little light to bear on that question. I knew, of course, as many others did that the Department of Justice had not approved use of deputy marshals. We discussed the propriety of using the Marine Corps Reserve component in Little Rock—most of whose members were local veterans and enrollees. Another possibility discussed was a request to be made of Lieutenant Governor Gordon to appeal for federal military assistance in suppressing a riot if real trouble should develop. Also one of the group mentioned that a small assignment of the Air Force Military Police (based twelve miles away) might be sufficient if they were legally available.

In August the President had said in a news conference in Washington that he could not conceive of a situation in which he would send federal troops into a state to enforce integration orders. For this reason, perhaps little thought had been given by anyone to the use of outside federal troops to supplement local forces. (Troops at Camp Chaffee, Arkansas, may have been mentioned in this conference but they were not thought of as importations, and anyway a request of the state government, temporarily under Lieutenant Governor Gordon's direction, for help was regarded as a condition to federal military assistance. There were many precedents for such help.) I am sure that no one in the group at that moment anticipated the dramatic and frightening appearance of paratroopers at Central High School within sixty hours.

To be sure, Harry Ashmore had persisted in the opinion

that the federal administration should consider no other military action than federalizing the National Guard and instructing them to comply with court orders. With the withdrawal at Christmastime of the last paratroopers, that is exactly what we had in Little Rock.

To all appearances, this Mayor's conference on Sunday was for the sole purpose of laying plans to prevent violence. The bitterest opponent of Mayor Mann could have found nothing to condemn in his expressed purposes (unless one wanted violence for the accomplishment of a desired end). No one in the group knew what Daisy Bates of the local NAACP proposed to do, and no one volunteered to advise her. The suggestion was made that Thurgood Marshall, representing the national NAACP, might still be in Little Rock and if contacted might be induced to counsel the nine to stay away for a few days. If the decision had been left with the Mayor's group that day, I believe they would have said, "Let them start tomorrow—a delay will give time to the extremists to build up for another demonstration and we will really have trouble." I had no strong opinion—the situation was so ominous that I merely wished the counsel of numbers. I agreed to use my Washington contacts to locate Thurgood Marshall in case it was decided that someone should seek his aid in averting disaster. This required more than one call, but I finally got his phone number in Richmond, Virginia. I did not call him and to my knowledge no others of the group did. The Mayor's deportment that Sunday was above criticism. Here was the greatest crisis he had ever faced, and as a "lame duck" he lacked the confidence of the people. I felt sorry for him.

In the late afternoon of that Sunday, Virgil Blossom met me in the Sam Peck lobby with this question: "Should I talk with Judge Davies about the necessity of having U.S. marshal's deputies accompany the nine Negro students into the Central High School?" I thought it would be proper in the unusual circumstances for him to approach the Judge. Within a few minutes he reported back to me that the Judge would not talk to him—he merely referred him to U.S. District Attorney Osro Cobb. Blossom then called Cobb but the District Attorney thought he would have to have specific authority from the Department of Justice to seek an order from the federal judge for United States marshal's deputies' help in protecting the Negro students. I called Sherman Adams to ask if he could get such clearance. This illustrates how determined I was to channel everything through Adams. I had brought him into the matter in the first place and I did not propose to bypass him or confuse the situation by multiple contacts, though I was sorely tempted to do so in order to spare him the discomfort of these continued appeals for information.

Adams called back to give me a telephone number at which Cobb could reach a responsible top official of the Department of Justice, adding that he thought the matter could be worked out. Some of the legal abracadabra seemed to annoy Adams, who is a businessman and definitely the executive type. Cobb told me that he did not get the authority from the department when he called that Sunday afternoon for further instructions as to Blossom's request for marshal's deputies to escort the Negro students. The local policemen (officers and men) had balked at "escorting." They pledged to do their duty in preventing violence if the Negroes showed up, but as to escorting—"No, don't ask that," and they meant it.

I knew Mr. Brownell's reasons for his ruling. He had publicly made much of the fact that Title III of the Civil Rights bill had been taken out by the Senate during the 1957 debate, and since that title was the one which proposed to give the Justice Department authority to participate in suits for enforcement of Negroes' rights, he construed the action as a legislative declaration that he, the Attorney General, should exercise no such authority. It was up to the judges of the district courts, he believed. Technically that may have been correct—it would take a court decision to make sure—but I believe that since the federal government was responsible for Mr. Blossom's predicament, the federal government should have acted affirmatively and imaginatively to protect him and to uphold its own court's orders with civil, not military, power. The court had invited the United States to be a party to the action restraining interference with the School Board Plan. Their failure to do so is the weak place in the Justice Department's case on Little Rock.

The city officials were still considering keeping the Negro children out until at least the next Thursday, so that inflamed passions could cool. But Acting Governor Gordon indicated that a detachment of state police would upon request be sent to the area, and this fact, coupled with Mayor Mann's confidence that the situation was manageable, soon led Virgil Blossom and the school board to make the fateful decision to go ahead with integration on Monday even without the availability of federal marshals. This was a courageous decision by the board, showing a determination not to weaken in the face of threats of violence, to teach all students according to legal requirements. The events that followed do not detract from the strength of purpose of a group which was not anxious for desegregation, but which had a deep and abiding respect for our legal heritage.

I shall not dwell long on the unfortunate occurrences of that tragic Monday. I shared the feelings of horror held by all law-abiding citizens when acts of violence took place at Little Rock Central High School.

After the nine Negro students had been spirited into the

school, by means of the side entrance while diversionary tactics were being employed at the main door, the huge crowd which had gathered at the school quickly got beyond control. It must be remembered that some of these people came from out of the city, while others were merely observers or parents of the children inside who were concerned about the situation but took no part in the action. Virgil Blossom called to say that it looked bad "outside" and asked me if federal troops would be called. Then the Mayor informed me that, while his public position was that things had gone "on schedule," he had received word from Chief Potts that fighting had broken out and that he needed about 150 soldiers as soon as possible. Being the only contact these responsible officials had with the White House at this moment, I felt it was my duty to relay their message. I called Sherman Adams and he commented cryptically, "That's all the information I need." By 11:00 A.M., I was quite nervous because Adams had not called back, indicating to me that the administration had no definite plans as yet. Blossom telephoned again and his voice was almost frantic as he asked: "Are the troops coming or aren't they?" As he saw it, "The safety of the children depends on it." Once more in my capacity as a communications bridge I tried to reach Adams to help Blossom find out if help was being sent in. Adams was away from Washington, "en route," and not available, but I finally managed to talk with the Cabinet Secretary, Maxwell Rabb. He did not know the answer to my question, but he promised not to delay in checking on the situation. By the time he called back to say, "The troops are not on their way," the Negro students had been removed from the school on Blossom's suggestion. Before I could relay Rabb's information to Blossom, he had requested that the Mayor take this action in anticipation of later federal protection for these students. What influence this had on the administration's decision actually to send in troops, after all, I do not know. In any event, it seemed likely that the local police did not have sufficient manpower to preserve order with Negro students in the school.

Sherman Adams and I talked to each other again later in the day and he said, "You and I can sign off now—it's in other hands, I guess." I inquired as to whom the Mayor should deal with, since, with me out of the picture, he needed a direct contact with federal authority. Sherman recommended Assistant Attorney General Bill Rogers, after he had conferred with Brownell himself. As for me, I never at any stage talked with Brownell, except at the Newport Conference, and I had no thoughts of doing so at this time. I was reassured, though, when Sherman added that, if I needed to talk to someone again, "Call me anytime." Thus, on the morning of Tuesday, September 24, my struggle to prevent federal use of troops came to an end.

Relman Morin, AP correspondent and Pulitzer Prize winner for his reporting of the Little Rock story, told me recently that he had good reason for believing that the Daisy Bates (NAACP) group had not intended to attempt to enter the Negroes in Central High on September 23, and that Governor Faubus was really surprised when he learned, at Sea Island, Georgia, of Monday's developments. How plans got changed remains as much a mystery to me as it does to Governor Faubus.

There were speculations as to what might have happened "if": If the Governor had not gone away, and if he had sent state police to patrol actively the school area (he had never said he would not); If it had not been a bright clear day (it had rained hard the two previous days); If the fire chief had responded to Mayor Mann's request for the use of the fire hose; If Judge Davies had ordered the United States marshal to assist the local police and add to his force of deputies; If there had been a permanent federal judge presiding who had been appointed from the district; and, If the situation had arisen after, instead of before, the new city-manager form of government had been installed.

Thus it was that a combination of factors conspired against the success of the move to integrate peacefully the nine Negro students. Presumably, it was decided to go ahead on Monday to avoid giving the extremists further time to build up sentiment against the moderate plan of integration, by holding additional meetings to be harangued by inflammatory, imported speakers. At a considerably later date, I was informed that even Attorney General Brownell might not have favored the use of troops to restore order, that final crushing blow to hopes for accord between the federal and state governments.

After issuing a proclamation asserting that he would "use the full power of the United States—including whatever force may be necessary—to prevent any obstruction of the law and to carry out the orders of the Federal Court," President Eisenhower ordered troops from the famed 101st Airborne Division at Fort Campbell, Kentucky, to go to Little Rock to see that integration at Central High School was carried out without further violence. At the same time, the Arkansas National Guard was federalized. On Wednesday, September 25, the nine Negro students attended school with the armed might of the United States Army protecting them from lawlessness. The soldiers were tough and efficient in seeing that no obstructions were permitted, and the crowd that gathered was quickly dispersed.

Much of a congressman's recess period is devoted to speechmaking, but the Little Rock experience played havoc with my plans in this respect. I was scheduled to speak to the Little Rock Lions Club (oldest in Lions International) on Wednesday following the arrival of federal paratroopers on Tuesday evening, and I discarded my notes to speak extemporaneously of the crisis facing our people. This was my own club and I had spoken many times to my fellow Lions in the thirty-three years I had been a member. Never before had I failed to exert myself to make them laugh. They were not surprised, though, when I plunged immediately into the most solemn discussion I have ever engaged in. Any laughter on that occasion would have had a hollow ring. They, too, were numbed by events.

I was among friends and they were aware of the loneliness I had experienced in the collapse of mediation efforts. I told them that I had not abandoned my natural optimism but that I had a new comprehension of the meaning of the word. I gave them William E. Barton's definition of optimism: "Optimism is such sorrowful discontent with the good we have accomplished as to give us joy in the search for something better."

Perhaps I could sympathize more fully than anyone with both the President and the Governor. My relations with each of them had been non-political, and since I had been privileged with an intimate view of their struggles with the problem, I felt impelled in presenting my own position to avoid any trace of condemnation of them. I could say with feeling that I had detected real pain in the President's expression and his words in announcing over television his decision to move troops into Little Rock. One can believe, as I do, that a better way could have been found and still not be interested in an assessment of blame. Close as I had been to the situation until a few hours before the President's action, I could not have all of the facts upon which to base a judgment. I knew that the moral and intellectual resources of our nation must be directed to avoid a recurrence. Other cities must be spared.

It was not easy for me to urge my audience to keep their

faith in orderly processes of law so that Little Rock itself could yet become a symbol for harmonious race relations. The words I used were carefully chosen:

There are many reasons why we must be calm and temperate in our judgments. The demands for change cannot be dismissed with the claim that agitators and outsiders are responsible for our troubles. I believe that the colored citizen is apt to live a happier life in Little Rock than in Chicago, for example, though I must speak with restraint here since this could easily be attributed to provincialism. I am confident that the distress of our city is but one symptom of a malaise that troubles the nation and the world. This could happen anywhere and considering our good record it is something that should not have happened to our city. We deserve better than this. As we weigh the differences between Chicago and Little Rock, whatever the irritations there—and they are great, for the problem of the colored man in the North has assumed large proportions—it must be conceded that in Chicago he has been relieved of the official stigma which remains where segregation is imposed by force of law.

I know that spokesmen for the Negro, the wisest and best among them, mean what they say when they indicate that they do not believe that progress for their people lies in the proposal to throw together in every classroom white and colored pupils just for the sake of putting them in proximity to each other as they study. This would be not only a meaningless innovation, but poor educational policy. If New York City cares to try it out—as apparently they wish to do—the experiment will doubtless have little value for us. Trusted Negro leaders do however expect us to take their viewpoint and their aspirations into account—they prefer that we stop doing things for them and begin doing things with them.

I shall not dwell upon the aspirations of the colored people. Certainly we cannot expect them to withhold demands that their constitutional rights be accorded them, or that they not be given the benefits of new laws designed to help them, even though the law might be exceedingly unpopular with their white friends and neighbors. The enforcement of law is not limited to popular laws. Constitutional forms are maintained only when people are completely dedicated to the ideal of law and order without reference to its impingement upon some cherished practices of their own.

In the first days of federal patroling at the high school, the citizens of Little Rock were not able to call upon civic consciousness for the facilities needed for recovery. We were all mentally exhausted. We were numbed by the events. Two or three days later, when I called Billy Graham in New York to talk about his previously announced plans to hold a meeting in Little Rock, I said, "Don't come now—the patient is in a state of shock. The 'no visitors' sign is on the door. The chaplain is needed and should be admitted, but come when the patient has recovered and can appreciate your ministrations." He fully agreed.

On their own initiative, Clyde Lowry and W. H. Sadler, both former presidents of the Chamber of Commerce, convened a meeting of all former presidents with W. M. Shepherd, who was president at the time. I was invited to sit with them. I spoke frankly regarding my conviction that regardless of how we might feel about the propriety of troops in our city to enforce a court order or about the order itself, we could make no progress toward a condition of restored order and civic stability unless the influence of Little Rock leaders was fully committed to the rule of law. Segregation or integration was not the issue in this situation. I had plenty of support. Only one of the twenty-six took issue with me and he was rather sharp in his condemnation of my position. But at the second (or perhaps the third) meeting, a short statement was agreed upon and every one of the conferees signed his name to the significant document, including the one who had so strongly taken issue with me. He had a deep feeling about the "sanctity of segregation," and he did not sign until he was convinced that the requirements of law and order lay outside that controversy. A temporary and informal committee was established to study the problem and to maintain consultations.

With the coming of federal troops there was a new focus of political controversy, but in the city of Little Rock itself people on both sides of the question relaxed a bit—fear of bloodshed had almost vanished.

Some enraged parents called to ask me to register a protest against the use of troops and to do what I could to restore the old order. It was not easy to convince some of them that matters had passed out of the hands of Congress. But at least I could, and did, pledge my best effort to seek a non-violent settlement of the matter and to give the people of Little Rock every opportunity to control their schools without any more interference than was justified under our Constitutional system. The Constitutional question seemed technical and perhaps irrelevant to some. I found satisfaction in the fact that strong segregationists called me. Some were old friends. I wanted to maintain a reputation for hearing both sides and to live up to my oft repeated promise to try to represent all of the people. It seemed shocking, I fear, to some that I would include the Negroes among those whose points of view I felt duty-bound to study. They are constituents, too, I reminded these friends. Some interpreted my attitude as fence straddling, an accusation one must live with when one's personal views are not altogether popular and one is trying to be persuasive and discreet. The virtue of forthrightness is easy to claim when the representative's views are popular—he may pound his fist when he utters them. I could honestly admit my opposition to integration by military force, but when I spoke in support of the courts, I met with some resistance.

My main concern was in appealing to the people convincingly to recognize the issue as court compliance, the rule of law against violence, and on that issue segregationists and integrationists could meet. It remains the paramount question.

During the month of September, no Negro voices were heard except those of NAACP leaders. The Negro community seemed to be in silent retreat and they have remained silent. Almost by default, Mrs. Daisy Bates, the local chairman, spoke for them. Her aggressiveness did not reflect the temperament of the majority of Little Rock Negroes, but her views on the school question obviously had their support. I did not hear from my old associates on the Urban League Board which I had helped organize as an effective social service agency during the 1930's.

Before our trip to Newport, I had received a telephone call from the head of the Negro Democrats, I. S. McClinton. He expressed the hope that he would have an opportunity later to present their views to me and that I would try to give a sympathetic interpretation of these views to Governor Faubus. The Democratic organization could not speak for the entire Negro population, however. It was apparent, too, that the NAACP had severe limitations in undertaking to represent the Negro community. The Negroes seemed unable to put forward the kind of leaders who could speak with their full confidence and with an authentic voice. There are such Negro leaders, but extremism among the Negroes had the same intimidating influence that it had with many of the white population, and they were not heard. I suppose that some of the responsibility for this situation rested on the white community. No efforts were made to help the Negroes put into leadership positions their most disciplined and wisest men and women. When a prosecution was begun a little while later under a city ordinance against NAACP officials, including a Negro Methodist minister, for what appeared to be technical violations, it only strengthened the position of the NAACP among Negroes.

"Mrs. Bates has no large personal following among our people," said one of the Negro ministers, "but this sort of thing drives them in masses into her camp."

The Negroes seemed eager at all times to appear to be just as friendly as ever with their individual white friends, but they stuck to their mental retreat and did not invite discussion. They were aware of the necessities of the situation, and there was a certain pathos in the severing of the pleasant contacts between individuals.

McClinton called in October to ask me to see a committee of his group to discuss the future. With him were a Baptist minister and a retired mail carrier. They made clear their determination to do all within their power to prevent violence. The Negro people, they said, were united in this. Further, they thought that the white people should know that the Negroes were also united in thinking that their rights as defined by the United States District Court should be protected, even if the troops had to stay. This meant that the nine students should continue in Central High. They hoped that the white people would not ask for troop withdrawal until it could be done with safety. I pointed out that the two races had a common interest here—if the school board kept the school open and obeyed court injunctions, both white and colored students should have adequate protection. This view is consistent with my opposition to military enforcement.

I believed these three men as to the unanimity of Negro opinion on desegregation of Central High. Later, professional poll takers confirmed this judgment with irrefutable proof produced by their comprehensive local survey. Skeptical white leaders were convinced. The question whether

Little Rock Negroes would seek mass integration is a different question.

The people of Little Rock were largely inarticulate during the early days of the presence of federal troops at Central High. I made no effort to find out what the administration had in mind as to withdrawal. No one could answer that question anyway.

We had witnessed violence and we breathed easier when strong men stood between our city's children and danger. (White parents shared these anxieties, of course. They knew that violence directed toward Negro children would expose all to danger.) I was a bit impatient during those days with some of the statements of partisans in other states who seemed to welcome a showdown. Had they known the extent of our anxieties I am sure they would have, in expressing their own convictions, omitted the "let's you and him fight" overtones. We were too close to violence to find any enjoyment in outbursts of that kind.

In one of the several huddles of the twenty-six Chamber of Commerce former presidents, Superintendent Blossom and the six members of the school board were invited to participate, and they did a superb job of informing us of the extreme difficulties facing the administrators and faculty under court orders to teach nine Negro students in what was historically the all white high school. Blossom spoke feelingly and convincingly. With a short dissertation on the local NAACP decision to rely on their legal rights, he dispelled any idea of an official closing of doors to the nine at that time, and his board sustained him. This, they argued, was the practical side of it. The board's critics have tried to interpret this consistent court compliance policy as a thrusting of integration upon the people of Little Rock against their wishes. The record will not support that charge, as later actions by the board proved.

The hours spent by the twenty-six on these talks were fruitful. These outstanding civic leaders gained new understanding of the educational, sociological, and legal phases of the problem. If some had not been convinced by newspaper editorials that yielding to extremists, by sending the Negroes home or closing Central High, would mean a strengthening of lawlessness, they were made fully aware of this point by Dr. Will Cooper, at that time chairman of the school board, and by Mr. Blossom. No one questioned for a moment that a majority of the people preferred the segregated schools. No one argued that the defeat by two of these directors of extremist opponents in a 1956 election carried any mandate to integrate. The issue appeared in clearer outlines every day: law and order as opposed to threats and pressures (chiefly from outside Little Rock).

Emerging community judgments were quickly recognized —the bayonets should come off those guns. It was an affront to the community that was not justified in the first place. Military men are tough and they do not take chances, but we did not like that aspect of the policing one bit. The bayonets did come off, and furthermore, the military men very quickly recognized that while it might be weeks, maybe months, before all troops could go home, the strong display of power was no longer called for.

With the withdrawal of the last of the regular troops about Christmastime and the assignment of the task to the federalized Guard units of our own Arkansas men in greatly reduced strength, there was considerably less feeling about "militarization."

The meetings of the twenty-six (they have never adopted a name nor taken any step toward formal organization) were occasionally devoted to related issues, such as the election of the governing board for the new city-manager form of government on November 5. All were eager to avoid the inclusion of the question of segregation in the election, so the month of October was a period of suspended judgment as to the next steps to be taken. Some sessions were solely to hear reports from those who were observing internal school conditions and to confer regarding measures to avoid a special session of the state's General Assembly, which would, unless the political climate changed, result either in closing Central High School altogether or penalties such as withdrawal of state aid. In view of the desire of some leading political figures who were quite indifferent to Little Rock's misfortune, there was every reason for our disquietude.

Modern cities have often been confronted with hostile political forces originating in non-urban areas and injustices have occasionally resulted from the willingness of some politicians to exploit sentiment against the "big city fellows." It is a good horse to ride if one is indifferent to what happens to the city people.

To meet this threat, the group sought the counsel of educational leaders who had a state-wide interest and influence. Governor Faubus himself listened to a subcommittee's appeal for a postponement or abandonment of plans for a special session. He was impressed. The subcommittee was of the opinion that a cooling-off period was necessary and that there was little likelihood of a satisfactory end to the problem if the initiative were left in federal or state hands.

This businessmen's group continued to function as an informal mechanism for arriving at the settlement of the differences through democratic legal processes. Anxious for a "new look" at the problem, it had early advocated that the school board petition the courts for a stay of compliance with the adopted schedule of integration. The subcommittee operated as a "task force" to deal with all interested parties, under the able leadership of Walter Guy and including Warren C. Bray, Clyde E. Lowry, Raymond Rebsamen, and

Sam Strauss, Sr. The stabilization of conditions remained its goal.

Of importance in understanding the city's difficulties is its geography. Little Rock's Negro population is located largely in the eastern and southern sections of the city. A part of this area is served by the Central High School. The Horace Mann High School was constructed recently for the Negro students and is located in the southeastern section. It is modern and well equipped. The Hall High School, also new and modern, is located in the northwestern section and serves what is often called "the silk stocking section." In political circles it is given its correct designation, "the fifth ward," and its character as a favored economic section is well known. Efforts have sometimes been made to sharpen for political purposes the cleavage between this section and the other voting precincts. Some of the parents, noting that the school board had been supported generally by the fifth ward residents, have complained: "Oh yes, they are protected. Hall High School will have no Negro students, so they will not help maintain segregation at Central High." The picture is blurred. Some of the most outspoken opponents of desegregation live in the fifth ward. Still it is true that the fifth ward vote, coupled with the heavy Negro vote in the east end, swung the municipal election in November for six of the seven Good Government League candidates, defeating the Citizens Council pro-segregation candidates. This is a rather rare combination. The Negro vote was almost unanimous against the Citizens Council candidates. In the neighborhoods where very few wealthy people live, the Citizens Council candidates ran ahead. Most of the territory served by Central High would be so described.

Before the Little Rock crisis, however, there seemed to be little interest manifested by the "favored" economic group in the school board's plans. Some of the fifth warders actually encouraged resistance. This uncertain sentiment was noted by the Governor before Newport.

The remainder of the year 1957 was a busy period for me. The Little Rock experience completely disrupted my fall schedule. My projected trip to South America for the Inter-American Affairs Subcommittee of the House Foreign Affairs Committee and the Baptist Foreign Mission Board was cancelled. I stayed in Little Rock until early in October devoting most of my time to helping explore ways of extricating ourselves from the unprecedented situation. My mail increased as a result of the worldwide publicity Little Rock had received, and my Baptist Convention duties, as President of the Convention since May, 1957, having been somewhat neglected, now required considerable time. Still I hoped for a few days of vacation. Scattered through the three remaining months, I managed to squeeze in one long week-end at Hot Springs and a few days in New York City. While there, I was asked by Dave Garroway to appear on his program. It gave me a chance to describe what was meant by the "moderate Southern" position. The mail, which had begun to decrease, picked up again. A time or two, statements lifted out of context would anger a few people in the South (occasionally elsewhere) and I would be busy with replies.

My church position made it necessary for me to take pains to state precisely in what respects I had acted as a congressman and to make clear that I had not projected our Convention into the Little Rock controversy. While in the East, I had other opportunities to reach important audiences, which I seized upon because I was anxious for the people outside Arkansas to know something of the complexities of our school situation. I also began to pick up my "Baptist circuit" commitments, speaking at the State Conventions of Illinois, Texas, Louisiana, Mississippi, and Arkansas during

October and November. The Baptists of Texas (constituting a sixth of our entire convention) heard me respectfully, almost enthusiastically, as I pleaded with them to point the way to moral leadership in the race difficulties. I was given a warm welcome in Louisiana. It was a little different in Mississippi. One of the leading dailies was very hostile to me, and two of the churches passed resolutions asking the State Convention to withdraw its invitation to me to speak at the annual meeting. Feelings of resentment over Little Rock events were intense throughout the state.

I waited for instructions from the State Convention. They said, "Come ahead." Late in the afternoon of the evening I was to speak, November 13, I flew into Jackson from Baton Rouge. There had been a steady rain nearly all day. At 8 P.M. it was raining furiously, but still there was scarcely a vacant seat in the auditorium. The church resolutions had made me a controversial figure for a moment and the people had become interested in "this Arkansas character."

It was a difficult position for me. I knew that the Baptist leaders were nervous, fearing that someone might try to lead part of the audience out of the building or embarrass me in some other way. I was eager, too, not to embarrass them. Only an out-and-out segregationist would be entirely respectable to the rank and file of Mississippians just at that time. My interest, of course, was in the issue of law and order —rather than the involved question of race relations. It was not the time and place to discuss Little Rock. Still I had something to say about our traditional Baptist concern for people—"for young people and old people, for rural people and city people, for working people and professional people, for poor people and well-to-do people, for neighboring people and far away people, for black people and white people."

I began with a reference to my work for the Department of Agriculture in the 1930's when I came to Mississippi to help their farmers with credit problems—"to buy a farm or repair a home, to paint the barn and to get a new pair of mules. It was then that I became acquainted with their special problems. I came to know and love the people of Mississippi."

In an attempt to win my audience, I used my best humor. One of the men on the platform told me he had spotted some in the audience who had come with definite hostility. They tried at first not to laugh at my stories but were soon joining the rest of the crowd in a friendly response to my efforts to be on good terms—for the sake of our church and its mission of reconciliation. "We can love each other as we pursue our differences."

When I returned to Little Rock on November 20, I spoke at a meeting of the State Chamber of Commerce and presented a plan to gain for the city and the entire South the "breather" so many of us thought necessary. My proposal was to introduce legislation in the next session of Congress that would encourage a suspension of judicial procedures while a complete study—a re-examination and a re-survey—of the Supreme Court's decision was made. That this approach met a recognized need became evident when it received a favorable response from many of the several hundred leaders from every part of Arkansas attending the meeting. One should keep in mind that the Governor had steadfastly held to the idea that time was the key to the solution—that delays in integration orders were essential. He continued to maintain that, in Arkansas, no state functionary should be compelled to support federal orders until the constitutionality of the interposition and other statutes approved by the people in 1956 was determined. (Test cases should also be tried, the Governor believed, to determine the validity of certain 1957 acts of the legislature.) Once this conflict in laws had been resolved, federal policy could be clarified in a manner that should be more acceptable to the South.

Because I believed that a spirit of conciliation had to be restored before a final solution could be found, I deplored the visits of outsiders to Little Rock to stir up trouble. Those who exhorted the people to encourage threats of violence were concerned only with their own selfish ends. One illustration of this policy was the statement of Roy Harris of Georgia at the Little Rock Capital Citizens Council meeting held on January 14, 1958. He told a cheering crowd, "Little Rock has Ike over a barrel. If the people of Little Rock stand pat and he is forced to keep troops here from now on, he soon will be the laughing stock of the nation and the world."

In February, the businessmen's group repeated its recommendation to the school board to petition the courts for a stay of compliance. Now that a new board of directors was governing the city in a dedicated and forthright manner, it was believed to be a suitable time to make public the position of the businessmen, which had been only privately maintained heretofore. The community leaders were all committed to law and order, but they believed the city deserved and could make a case for further exploration of steps necessary to comply with court orders. The time was ripe for further judicial action, since the appointment of a new federal judge for Arkansas was imminent and, in any case, it seemed likely that Judge Davies would no longer be responsible for hearing the appeal. In light of the New Orleans Court of Appeals decision delaying integration in Dallas, the school board was urged "to develop its case fully so it could properly appeal should the decision be adverse in the lower court."

The school board now decided to follow the advice of the businessmen's group and ask for a postponement of integration until: (1) the concept of "all deliberate speed" could be defined clearly and (2) effective legal procedures for integrating the schools could be developed in a manner that would not impair the quality of the educational program. Said the petition: "The District, in its respect for the law of the land, is left standing alone, the victim of extraordinary opposition on the part of the State Government and apathy on the part of the Federal Government." In a surprisingly strong but well-warranted tone of indignation, the board outlined the record of interference that its plans had met and the frustrations it had felt, pleading for judicial understanding of its problems.

It was in this context that I introduced, on March 6, my bill calling for the establishment of a Joint Committee of the Congress to study the results of the Supreme Court decisions on school desegregation. In the statement I issued, I pointed out:

> There is great need to re-examine the situation in the South in the light of the difficulties growing out of edicts requiring sudden change in age-old customs of the people. . . . The Committee would be called upon to suggest to all school districts various alternative ways of complying with the order to desegregate that would do the least violence to local customs and attitudes. The Jeffersonian principle of considering local variations in conditions should be embraced in the national policy and this is one way to bring that about. . . . I hope that this proposal will help assure the South that haste and force will not prevail, but rather that patience and tolerant understanding of the problems in all sections will be achieved. It is only in this way that we can stimulate throughout the region the moral fervor and racial good will that have been characteristic of the South.

Thus the forces of moderation in Little Rock were rallying to encourage the people of the city to stick to their traditional devotion to the law while at the same time calling on the national community to have patience and forbearance. That this was not an easy road to travel was quickly revealed by the immediate reaction to the introduction of my bill. While many Southern newspapers gave me a fair hearing and some even praised me for championing the Southern cause, others denounced me as betraying my heritage by becoming an avowed integrationist. At the same time, Clarence Mitchell of the NAACP, whom I had previously held to be pretty levelheaded in his championing of equal rights for Negroes, accused me of "trying to turn back the clock of integration." At the tenth annual conference of the National Civil Liberties Clearing House, he said that my action was "a repudiation of everything the Christian Church stands for" and that I was unworthy of leading a church group. The intensity of the feelings expressed by both extremes proved once again that the path of moderation was not "the easy way out." I was grieved at the bitter attacks but even more determined to stick to a course that I believed provided the only hope for lasting racial peace.

On March 21, Sherman Adams asked me to come to the White House to confer again regarding the Central High School situation. In the earlier calls I had made on Sherman during the first Eisenhower administration, I had often given him "a new Arkansas story"; generally he asked for one. Since September, however, there were few moments of levity in our conversations.

On this occasion Sherman came to the point quickly. "Get Secretary Brucker on the phone," he said to his secretary, and we had a three-way talk. The Secretary explained what they had in mind about ultimate withdrawal (before June) of all the troops from the high-school building, leaving only a few men stationed at Camp Robinson across the river. Adams asked me to prepare the city and school authorities for this gradual "phasing out" of the force at the school building, leaving the policing at that point to the local authorities. This was a consummation I had devoutly hoped for—the complete withdrawal of the military—though I had never recommended it until all who had a right to be consulted were sure that it would not jeopardize the safety of Negro or white students. I called Josh Shepherd and Clyde Lowry, members of the businessmen's group, asking them to consult the school board and the Mayor and to give me the composite judgment as to this proposed next step. Shepherd called on behalf of the group, at the end of the six-man meeting which lasted an hour and a half, to say that the reaction was negative, that the city was not ready for withdrawal of all the men from Central High. I was familiar enough with the situation not to require a detailed statement of the reasons. Lowry and Shepherd, having opposed the use of the military from the outset, were as eager as I to see the troops withdrawn, but recognized that the new city-manager government was simply not ready to assume such solemn responsibility.

Sherman was terribly disappointed. He raised his voice: "Now what will they do when we finally *have* to pull out— soldiers can't stay there indefinitely—the city must be prepared some day to do ordinary policing."

I could not deny that, neither could he deny that timing was too important to be disregarded. Once during the conversation, to keep the talk from getting too brusque, I said, "You and I are about to get into an argument—that doesn't make sense. We both want the same thing—the troops out!" He gave a quick assent, saying he was not irritated—just anxious for us to make progress. I recalled to him that one time previously he had said, when we had been able to forecast a course that would ease tension and avoid the strain on federal-state relations, "We must work our way out of this together." We both moralized a bit following that comment. "It's bound to come out all right eventually," I said, and Sherman then referred to the belief of his Baptist preacher grandfather that "all things work together for good." He then outlined another more gradual course of troop withdrawal which seemed practical.

It was ironic, though, that at this juncture the White House wanted no troops at Central High, while the local leaders wanted them (the minimum). I admired Sherman and sympathized with him, too, knowing that he had many other headaches in addition to this one.

I did not see him again till after Easter. At home during the recess I learned from talks with the leaders that the second plan was working. On April 15, the one day I spent in Washington before leaving for Moscow for the four-day visit with Russian Baptists, there was time to talk with him over the phone. I was glad to give him a summary of favorable changes in sentiment at home during the six weeks preceding Easter. The extremists had "overegged their pudding," I told him. The chairman of the school board, Wayne Upton, had said, "I would rather lose the School Board's law suit for a review and change of the desegregation order than to have a part in forcing retention of troops here past the time when they could be safely removed."

Never at any time following the September 23 conversation in which he said, "You and I will sign off," had Adams and I discussed the administration's decision with reference to the use of troops, but there was no cause for exchanging views on that point. Differing as I did with the White House in essential particulars of that decision, I nevertheless gave Sherman credit for desiring as much as I a solution that would get the responsibility for law and order firmly placed with state and local authorities.

Only once in the talks we subsequently had on the subject did I say anything about past mistakes, and it was a repetition of my opinion that the Department of Justice should have permitted United States Attorney Cobb to discuss with the federal judge the assignment of a few deputies from the marshal's office to help the city police maintain order on September 23. It would not have been fair to my friend to ask for details as to decisions not to use United States marshals and the later decision to use troops.

It was shortly after this that the appeal of Governor Faubus from the injunction issued by Judge Davies against his use of the National Guard to keep Negro children out of Central High was denied by the United States Circuit Court of Appeals. This court ruled that the state could not use its forces to suppress "rights which it is the duty of the state to defend." If such use were permitted, it would encourage violence, since opponents of those rights would have the expectation of the support of the forces of law so long as they gathered in sufficient numbers to constitute a menace to life. In the opinion of this three-man court, "a rule which would permit an official whose duty it was to enforce the law to disregard the very law which it was his duty to enforce in order to pacify a mob or suppress an insurrection, would deprive all citizens of any security in the enjoyment of their life, liberty and property."

It was at this stage in developments that Herbert L. Thomas, Sr., a Little Rock insurance executive, began sponsoring a plan to solve the integration stalemate on a voluntary basis outside the courts. He had been a member of the Board of Trustees of the University of Arkansas when it became the first Southern state university to admit Negro students to the law and medical colleges without being required by law suit to do so. He stressed obedience to the courts but advocated voluntary state action which would remove the cause for court involvement. Both sides to the controversy would have to agree to: (1) the organization of a state bi-racial commission to help each school district make its own definition of "all deliberate speed" and then execute it, and (2) the withdrawal of the Negro students from Central High after school closed at the end of May. After an early flurry of active interest on the part of both supporters of Governor Faubus and prominent Negro leaders, hopes for the plan soon waned and its chances for acceptance became remote. Josh Shepherd, a member of the businessmen's group, organized the Committee for the Arkansas (Thomas) Plan in the hope that moderates would rally around this new banner and soon convince all parties that the moral persuasion on a state-wide basis envisaged by Mr. Thomas was the best way to end bitterness and strife. To date, neither side has seen fit to agree to this approach.

With the school year rapidly approaching an end, President Eisenhower, in early May, ordered the withdrawal of all federal troops from Central High after school closed. In his statement releasing the remaining Guardsmen on May 29, he said: "Following that date I trust that State and local officials and citizens will assume full responsibility and duty for seeing that the orders of the Federal court are not obstructed. The faithful execution of the responsibility will make it unnecessary for the Federal Government to act further to preserve the integrity of our judicial processes."

The withdrawal of troops ended a chapter in the Little Rock story. The rest of the story is a part of still unfolding history that must wait for the telling. But however the story may conclude, the rule of law must prevail.

CHAPTER SEVEN

The Resources of Faith

IN THE LAST ANALYSIS, IT WILL BE THE CHURCHES AND THE local community organizations that will provide solutions to the problems of civil rights. Like the large majority of Southerners, white and Negro, my upbringing had a strong religious accent, and I have been an active church member all my life. I have also enjoyed working with secular organizations in behalf of intergroup harmony and the American ideals of brotherhood and justice.

In my early Arkansas days, as I have already pointed out, I was one of the organizers of the Little Rock Chapter of the Urban League. In 1925 I began teaching the Bible Class of the Second Baptist Church in Little Rock, which has since paid me the great honor of adopting my name, and in 1929 I was chairman of the First Rural Church Commission of the Arkansas Baptist Convention. I have served as one of the directors of the Little Rock YMCA and the Arkansas Tuberculosis Association, and I was president of the Arkansas Children's Home and Hospital. From 1932 to 1935 I was president of the Arkansas Conference of Social Work.

After my arrival in Washington, I became identified with such organizations as the National Policy Committee and the Commission on Interracial Cooperation. As vice-chairman of the National Policy Committee, I took leave of absence from the Farm Security Administration to make a four-months' tour of the Southern states. This project was under the immediate direction of the Southern Policy Association of which I was vice-president. This group had been organized for the purpose of studying all aspects of the South's economic and social life, with special attention devoted to the tenancy situation. The purpose of my tour was to interpret to groups affiliated with the association the meaning of the democratic process in the formulation of public policy and to discuss the political and social objectives to which the democratic process points.

My participation in these outside activities underwent a necessary transition when I entered the United States Congress. My work with the Commission on Interracial Cooperation came to an end at the same time the organization itself underwent a gradual evolution. The impetus for this new direction came partly from the Durham (N.C.) Conference of October, 1942, made up of influential Negroes from all sections of the South. Their historic declaration became known as the "Durham Statement." World War II had focused the attention of minorities upon the need for asserting their rights, and this document was an eloquent plea for justice and fair treatment. While it called for the protection of the right to vote, the abolition of the poll tax, a strong FEPC, and many other civil rights measures, it acknowledged that equality of educational opportunities rather than school mergers was the best that could be hoped for at the time, recognized the strength "of the legal and customary patterns of race relations," and called upon "all fair-minded men to evolve in the South a way of life consistent with the principles for which we as a nation are fighting throughout the world, that will free us all, white and Negro alike, from want, and from throttling fears."

Southern white people interested in bettering race relations could not ignore this call to interracial cooperation, and three hundred people signed the Atlanta reply, drafted on April 8, 1943, by prominent citizens of ten states. While not making a complete reply to the issues raised, these influential Southerners agreed that "these Negro leaders rightly placed emphasis in their statement on discrimination in the administration of our laws on purely racial grounds.... No Southerner can logically dispute the fact that the Negro, as an American citizen, is entitled to his civil rights and economic opportunities." The Atlanta statement went on to "agree with the Durham Conference that it is 'unfortunate that the simple efforts to correct obvious social and economic injustices continue, with such considerable popular support, to be interpreted as the predatory ambition of irresponsible Negroes to invade the privacy of family life.' We agree also that 'it is a wicked notion that the struggle by the Negro for citizenship is a struggle against the best interests of the nation. To urge such a doctrine, as many are doing, is to preach disunity, and to deny the most elementary principles of American life and government.' "

The statement closed with a call to the South to organize to solve its race questions, because "it is futile to imagine or to assert that the problem will solve itself. The need is for a positive program arrived at in an atmosphere of understanding, cooperation, and a mutual respect." While I was not one of the signers, because of my Congressional obligations, I was much in sympathy with this new movement and watched with great interest as a third conference grew out of the first two. The eight people who met in Richmond, Virginia, on June 16, 1943, were a joint committee of representatives of the Durham and Atlanta conferences, this meeting differing from the previous ones by being bi-racial and composed of delegated individuals.

The resolutions of this committee cited "finding common ground for universal action and balanced harmony among all peoples" as "the world's greatest need and hope." They went on to say that "this is the problem of two great peoples caught up in the midst of transition between the powerful heritage of the past and the mighty pull of the future." After listing the areas of possible improvement of civil rights, the signers urged the continuation of this committee, to be charged with "the responsibility for working out methods and practical means of approach," urging the public "to a new sense of the meaning of these needs as they accord with our professed principles of Christianity and democracy." As an outgrowth of these resolutions, the Collaboration Committee appointed twenty-two white persons and nineteen Negroes to a new committee, which resolved itself into the Southern Regional Council. The co-chairmen, Charles S. Johnson and Howard W. Odum, proceeded with plans to perfect the organization. Thus came into being an outstanding agency active in working for race harmony and carrying into its literature and methods an emphasis reflecting the region's religious tradition.

Several years after the Southern Regional Council was organized, I had the opportunity of debating Dr. Johnson, then president of Fisk University, on the Town Hall Meeting of the Air. The subject of our discussion on April 8, 1950, was: "What Effect Do Our Race Relations Have on Our Foreign Policy?" Dr. Johnson, a distinguished Negro educator, based his argument on the "handicap under which our own diplomatic representatives must work in negotiating with other nations, friendly and unfriendly, when this specter of race is introduced." He called our racial system "the Achilles' heel of both our domestic and foreign policy." The racial difficulties in Washington, D.C., were cited as excellent propaganda material for the Communists, since Negro foreign dignitaries were likely to see at first hand evidences of our policy of segregation and discrimination. He closed with this observation: "We are before the bar of world opinion as the chief advocate of the right of individuals to live as free men, equal before the law. Unless we can solve our own racial problems we cannot hope to plead success-fully the cause of freedom and equality for others."

In my initial comments, I pointed out that my differences with Dr. Johnson were primarily a matter of emphasis and added, "I would highlight the tremendous progress already made. He insists that the imperfections be emphasized." To back up my argument, I asked my audience to remember, "It is not an idle boast that nowhere in the world has any minority group experienced the advances which have been registered by the Negro people of the United States within the past fifty years. Contrasted with many situations in the Old World, it should be convincing evidence that we do believe in social justice and equality of opportunity." It was my belief that we should place this progress in the foreground of every discussion of race relations and foreign policy.

With regard to the specific objections to America's racial conduct that were raised by Dr. Johnson, I replied that efforts to change that conduct "must be reviewed in the light of Constitutional principles." "Under the American system," I reminded him, "many decisions must be made by the states, not by the federal government, which determines foreign policy." Recalling Dr. Johnson's previous activities, I said that I was sure that "this was the thought of the Negro leaders who framed the Durham Conference Statement of 1942, to the effect that progress must be within the frame-work of our democracy."

During the question period following our addresses, I was asked: "Is America building a foreign policy on issues which it does not intend to tolerate here in America?" This was my reply: "I hope not. We could certainly not sustain such a policy. We must build our policy in good faith upon those foundation principles of our government in the great documents of the past in which we believe, in the Declaration of Independence, in the Constitution of the United States. If we deviate from these principles for strategy reasons abroad, then we will fail.

"That bears out, I think, what I said a moment ago: It's one problem after all. We must prove our good faith by our achievements at home. I think we are proving it. I think we are making tremendous progress."

Anyone who doubted this progress need only have attended the annual meeting of the Southern Baptist Convention in St. Louis from June 3 to 5, 1954. (My activities in the Convention had continued to be numerous throughout my public life, and in 1951 I had been honored by being elected second vice-president. I shall give attention to this Convention's work in improving race relations only because of my identification with it as a Southern Baptist, and I do not wish to diminish in any way the importance of the great work done by other denominations and faiths in this same area.) At this meeting, its Christian Life Commission made a detailed presentation of its achievements. I would like to deviate briefly to indicate the nature of this important Baptist agency. It is based primarily on the responsibility of all Christians to apply the teachings of Christ to human society. As the Commission puts it, "the Christian treatment of his brother in business, industry, politics, race or any other relationship cannot be passed off as a social matter for which he has no responsibility." Its members elected by the Southern Baptist Convention, the Commission seeks to re-examine the Christian's responsibility in human affairs as in economic life, industrial relations, racial understanding, citizenship, world affairs, and other vital issues. It also helps inform and mobilize our Christian forces against the destructive forces of alcoholic beverages, obscene literature, gambling, juvenile crime, the traffic in narcotics, and many other social evils. The devices employed to achieve these ends are: (1) the development and distribution of an informational and interpretive literature; (2) summer conferences at state and Southern Baptist assemblies; (3) Christian Life conferences in churches; and (4) cooperation with state and associational committees on social service, temperance, or civic righteousness.

At the Convention in 1954, the most important subject that the Christian Life Commission reported on was the recent Supreme Court decision on school segregation. Here is its language:

In the light of the recent decision handed down by the Supreme Court of our nation declaring segregation of the races in the public schools to be unconstitutional, and in adhering to the basic moral principles of our religion as they apply in race relations, we recommend:

1. That we recognize the fact that this Supreme Court decision is in harmony with the constitutional guarantee of equal freedom to all citizens, and with the Christian principles of equal justice and love for all men.

2. That we commend the Supreme Court for deferring the application of the principle both as to time and procedure until the nation shall have had time to work out methods by which transition from the present practice may be effected.

3. That we urge our people and all Christians to conduct themselves in this period of adjustment in the spirit of Christ; that we pray that God may guide us in our thinking and our attitudes to the end that we may help and not hinder the progress of justice and brotherly love; that we may exercise patience and good will

in the discussions that must take place, and give a good testimony to the meaning of Christian faith and discipleship.

4. That we express our belief in the public school system of our nation as one of the greatest factors in American history for the maintenance of democracy and our common culture, and we express the hope that in the working out of necessary adjustments, its place in our educational program shall not be impaired.

5. That we urge Christian statesmen and leaders in our churches to use their leadership in positive thought and planning to the end that this crisis in our national history shall not be made the occasion for new and bitter prejudices, but a movement toward a united nation embodying and proclaiming a democracy that will commend freedom to all peoples.

While I did not agree fully with the conclusions of this statement, I was in wholehearted support of its appeal for "patience and good will in the discussions that must take place," relying on divine guidance in our thinking and our attitudes to lead us to "justice and brotherly love."

The following year, I was elected chairman of the Commission. During that time, in the spring of 1956, there was issued "An Appeal for a Christian Spirit in Race Relations," signed by twenty-eight Southern Baptist leaders. It responded to the rising tensions in race relations as follows:

In response to a request from the Advisory Council for Work with Negroes—a group of workers serving with various agencies in Southern Baptist life—we have been given the opportunity to express our personal convictions about this matter.

We are speaking as individuals, desiring to witness for Christ, and have no thought of speaking for Southern Baptists or for any church or agency affiliated with the Southern Baptist Convention.

We appeal to our Baptist brethren, white and Negro, and to other Christian friends, to give careful consideration to the following statement of principles, setting forth, we believe, the truth of the Bible and offered in the spirit of good will and Christ in love.

1. God created man in his own image. Therefore, every man possesses infinite worth and should be treated with respect as a person.

2. Christ died for all men. Therefore, the Christian view of man, every man, must reflect the spirit of the cross.

3. God is no respecter of persons. Therefore, prejudice against persons or mistreatment of persons on the grounds of race is contrary to the will of God.

4. Christ said, "Thou shalt love thy neighbor as thyself." Therefore, Christians are obligated to manifest active good will toward all people and to help them to achieve their fullest potentialities as persons.

5. Christian love, as exemplified by Christ, is the supreme law for all human relations. Therefore, Christians have the assurance that such love, conscientiously practiced, will resolve tensions and bring harmony and good will in race relations.

6. All true Christians are brothers in Christ and children of God. Therefore, they are obligated to cultivate prayerful concern for one another and to show confidence in one another.

7. Every person is accountable to God. Therefore, the right of individual opinion, tested by the teachings of Christ, and of freedom to express it, always in the spirit of Christian love, should be granted to all and respected by all.

We commit ourselves to seek new insights as to our Christian duty and to seek more grace in manifesting Christian love toward all men. We earnestly appeal to others to join with us in making this commitment and in the resolve to pray unceasingly that the Spirit of God will help us to create a fellowship that will be a witness for Christ to all peoples and all races around the world.

In conjunction with this cry for Christian tolerance, the Christian Life Commission reported to the Convention, meeting in Kansas City in April, its desire to support the awakening of the submerged peoples of the world to their personal destinies and inherent freedoms. We were proud to realize that wherever the Christian gospel has been preached it has awakened in the people "a sense of their dignity and worth and has set them straining at the shackles of their bondage." We made this call to "the courage of prudence":

In view of our responsibility as a major group of world Christians we must be mature enough in our faith and strong enough in our fellowship to face with forthright sincerity the issues among us that vitally affect our gospel witness at home and around the world. There is no reason for us to avoid these issues or couch them in evasive language or sentimental speech. The hard realities of our present situation demand honesty, integrity and a humble sense of responsibility. Our tragic situation calls for courage, but it should be the courage of prudence and of intelligent conviction.

With such courage and conviction we must face the present controversy in our relations with the Negro people. On this issue we are divided in opinion but let us not be divided in fellowship. No one person or group has the wisdom to lead us to a solution of the difficult situation that has developed. Only God in his infinite love and patience can do that. The times call for prayer and deep humility. They call us to repentance toward God and to confessions for hate and hasty words toward our fellowman.

The times call us none the less to meet this issue as Christians should. We must meet it with facts and scriptural truth. We must recognize the fact that the problem of race relations in America is rooted deeply in our history and is the product of a series of tragic social experiences that have left their marks on both our groups.

These deep-rooted social attitudes do not easily die. In some areas there can be no quick solution. And those who hope to achieve a peaceful adjustment must gird themselves with patience. The white man should seek to subdue the pride of his old mastery, the Negro the pride of his new achievement.

The Christian cannot stop at the point of law. He is motivated by love and grace. In spite of all the hate that has been shown and the hasty words that have been spoken Christian people must move into this controversy to accomplish friendly and mutually helpful adjustments.

When I was asked to continue as chairman of the Commission for another year, I decided to accept, because I was fully aware of the need to push forward the doctrines of the brotherhood of man and the triumph of justice and mercy with whatever influence my voice might have. In this determination, I was encouraged by the following statement in the Information Service Bulletin of the National Council of the Churches of Christ, paying tribute to our own executive director, Dr. A. C. Miller: "The Christian Life Commission of the Southern Baptist Convention, under able and wise leadership, is at work among the local churches, seeking to enlist their leadership in efforts to prevent threats of violence." The paragraph went on to point out that "they have prepared and sent out some of the most effective materials, aimed at correcting appeals to Scripture in support of segregation. They have stood firm in support of public education and of Constitutional government. At this meeting, the budget of the Commission is infinitesimal in a constituency of 30,000 local churches. But the light of this Commission is shining, and all the darkness cannot put it out." In this regard, I told my brethren in my acceptance speech that the Negro's situation might be likened to his being in a cave. While he might not be able to emerge immediately, no blocks must be thrown in his way. He must be able to see the light ahead, and it must be our job to assist him in putting away the stones that lie in his path and block the light.

It was not long after my return to Washington from this Convention that concern over civil rights reached a fever pitch in Congress. After much soul-searching, as described in Chapter IV, I signed the Southern Declaration of Principles of the hundred congressmen and senators objecting to the Supreme Court school decisions. I was fully aware that this action would cause much consternation among my church acquaintances, but that did not relieve the pain when the angry reactions began to arrive in my daily mail. The great debate which raged in the state of Arkansas was reflected in my own conscience and heart. Despite the reasons I have given for my support of the Manifesto, I found it difficult to take issue with the Supreme Court and the ethical doctrines of my church organizations.

This fact was uppermost in my mind when I returned to Arkansas for two weeks of campaigning between adjournment of Congress on July 31 and the primary for my re-election on August 14, 1956. I had already received word that the Negro people of my district resented deeply my signing the Manifesto. A delegation of Negro leaders presented a "Declaration of Christian Principles" to a meeting of The Arkansas Citizens for Orderly Compliance, saying that "the Court's decision is in harmony with Christian theology and ethics and churchmen in local communities should give leadership in planning for implementing the decision and in the difficult task of preparing people for the transition." This declaration went on to claim:

If it is God's will to have the intimate fellowship of eternity with all peoples, then God's mandate to us in Arkansas is clear. We are to have fellowship with all his children regardless of differing racial characteristics. Realistically there is no way short of civil war to circumvent permanently the Supreme Court decision. At best there are only measures which presumably would prolong the period of transition until declared unconstitutional. A three-judge federal court has already declared one state's assignment bill unconstitutional. Undoubtedly all such evasion of justice will meet the same fate. Such legislative gimmicks which have been passed in other states tend only to give racists a false hope, to inflame bitter controversy among the people, and to thwart an orderly and peaceful compliance with the law of the land. . . . We believe our Arkansas Congressional representatives to have done the people of our State a disservice in labeling the Supreme Court decision as "a clear abuse of judicial power." In no way do we believe that the Court has encroached upon the "reserved rights of the states".... To defend segregation on the basis of states' rights is neither politically defensible nor morally justifiable. ... As Arkansas approaches the time for election of public officials we wish to warn the people against any candidate who makes the issue of race the paramount issue of his campaign. There are many issues which face us as responsible citizens. They must not be overshadowed by centering attention upon racial animosity. Any candidate should automatically be suspect of evil designs against the public who centers his campaign around racial fears and prejudices....

The final statement of their "compliance" organization, made up of both Negroes and whites, was more moderate and conciliatory, pledging its members to "orderly compliance" with the Supreme Court order but "not demanding immediate integration in every community." The constitution of this group did re-emphasize its belief that enforced segregation of the races is contrary to Christian belief and democratic principles. I was, of course, not intending to base my campaign on matters of race and did indeed address myself primarily to the issues of federal aid for school construction, rural industrialization, multi-purpose development of the Arkansas River, achievement of world peace, and other matters of national and international concern. Nevertheless, I knew that the Negro people were now quite perplexed, in the light of my past record on race questions. In 1942, when I was first elected to Congress, there had been some criticism of my being too friendly to the minority race and too enthusiastic in promoting their progress. This and other aspects of my political past had given me a rather firm hold on the Negro voters and I took some pride in the fact, especially since they had the privilege of voting for the first time shortly after my election. I knew, however, that it would not help me appreciably to describe to them the soul-searching that preceded my action in joining the other Arkansas members of Congress in signing the Manifesto, nor would it be of much interest to them that I had refused to sign the original draft which had, among other objectionable features, an approval of interposition. "It was a time to stand up and be counted," they had concluded, and they were virtually unanimous in condemning all of the Southern congressmen who signed it. I knew also that, in support of this sentiment, they had some eloquent spokesmen among the white people. While such comments as I have already reported pained me somewhat, they were welcome evidence that there was an alert interest in protecting minority rights. For after all, it is from this core of good will and independence in scattered places in the South that the influences will come to produce the sentiment necessary to achieve minimum standards of justice.

One of my most rewarding meetings during the 1956 campaign was the open conference with the Negro ministers of Little Rock, at which my opponent was also present. They came to the point quickly. The pastor of one of Little Rock's largest Negro churches, a respected leader in interracial movements, spoke caustically: "Mr. Hays, I simply cannot understand how a man with your background in good race relations could fail to maintain a high moral position. And may I say, sir, when someone does something to weaken the Constitution of the United States and the law of the land, though he be my own brother, I could not feel friendly toward him." Others spoke as vigorously.

It was a moving experience for me. I recalled, as their excoriations were advanced, how they had until recently been denied all such outlets. When my turn to speak arrived, I emphasized one heartening fact.

Before defending myself, I want to point out that the significant thing about this meeting is that you are "putting me in my place."

You are criticizing a white man to his face and doing it forcibly. You are confronting your representative with expressions of dissatisfaction just as my other constituents have always been free to do. And it is my philosophy that this is necessary for the proper functioning of the representative system of government. But even as recently as three years ago you could hardly have done this. You would not have felt free to do it. You have been enfranchised. You are able to confront me. That is good, and I am so impressed by it that I cannot muster the mental energies to make a defense of myself on the Manifesto issue. You might be right about that matter. There were arguments on both sides. I did what I thought would serve the common interest. I could not convince you of that, so I will only suggest that we do all we can to keep our bridge of understanding between the races intact and try to get rid of the present tensions.

Their silence was louder than their speeches had been. It was evident, now that I had called their attention to it, that they were aware of the tremendous change during the last few years.

It was at this point that an old friend and former president of a Negro college told the gathering the story I later repeated to Adlai Stevenson in Chicago at the Democratic Convention, the story of the minister who had "slipped before and then gotten back on the right track." My final argument was the reminder that the right to condemn a Supreme Court decision was what had enabled them to gain the judicial advantage they now held. Viewed in this light, the Manifesto could not be regarded as an unconstitutional document. I pointed out that our honest disagreements could be reconciled on the basis of social, religious, and political actions of an educational nature, rather than by the utilization of the coercive powers of government, be they executive, legislative, or judicial. In maintaining this view I was putting into practice the Baptist doctrines of my belief, recognizing the obligation to urge my fellow citizens to take the actions necessary for a final reconciliation.

In May of 1957, at the Southern Baptist Convention in Chicago, I was elected president of the Convention. This, of course, was the culmination of my religious life and work. Feeling very deeply the issues facing the Baptist people in the South, I told the Executive Committee in my initial meeting with them: "You may have a controversial president on your hands. Knowing how you feel about controversy in a group as large as ours, with its diversity of views and interests, of political philosophies and economic and social attitudes, I can understand how this might be a rather frightening reference. I hope I shall not embarrass you. I assure you I shall not invite controversy, but I am determined to be my natural self and I may be drawn into controversy merely by doing what I regard as my duty to you. But please look at it this way. It would be better for me to be controversial because of a conviction than to avoid controversy in a way that would give you *cause* to be ashamed of me."

These prophetic words were more accurate than I realized. My role as mediator in the Little Rock crisis, four months later, made me a more controversial figure than I desired or intended to be. That the Southern Baptists were prepared to support my right to do as my conscience dictated was confirmed by my re-election to a second term as president in May, 1958. This was an affirmation of my Christian duty to act according to my own judgment in an issue of crucial importance to religious people, not necessarily a sign of approval of the position I had taken. What was significant in that regard was the overwhelming defeat of a move to reject the Christian Life Commission report, "A Call for Racial Reconciliation," which called for strengthened "fellowship with people of every race."

It is important that I make clear that I was not acting in

my capacity as president of the Convention when I arranged
the Newport Conference. When Governor Faubus and I
were at the Little Rock airport, ready to take off for Newport
on September 13, I was asked by one of the reporters, "Does
your office as president of the Southern Baptist Convention
have anything to do with your activity in this situation?"
Before I could answer, he added apologetically, "If that is a
mean question, please don't blame me. My city editor told
me to ask it." It was easy to answer. "No," I said. "It is altogether a governmental matter. Don't forget that no Baptist
can speak for eight and a half million Baptists. No Baptist
can speak for two Baptists." But as the crisis dragged on, I
saw that I had a triple role: I was attempting to mediate (a
function that will become increasingly important as efforts
continue to define precisely the respective functions and
powers of state and federal authority); I was acting in my
capacity as a congressman; and partly because I was a
Baptist official, I found that the role of moralist was inescapable.

The prominent role of the church in this process should
be welcomed. Baptist conventions cannot bind individual
churches, and sentiment in many places where there is great
Baptist strength is largely opposed to change. Many ministers are under pressure not to speak on race issues at all,
but even they may be helpful in creating a better atmosphere
where extremists have been spreading the propaganda that
the Bible teaches segregation.

I have listened to ministers of my own denomination discuss the problem of how to supply moral and spiritual guidance in race matters in congregations of strong segregationist sentiment. Many ministers are confronted by a difficult
task; they obviously cannot conduct a frontal attack. That
course would cost them the opportunity to influence their
congregations. In some areas they would even lose their

pulpits by pleading too patently for "moderation" (to some, moderation is synonymous with integration). Still they have a useful function in furthering the service of "reconciliation," urging people to love each other as they differ. I was pleased with the response in Georgia and elsewhere to my suggestion in an Atlanta interview that Baptists do three things: (1) seek a non-violent solution, (2) avoid economic, political, or social pressures upon the preachers to prevent their saying what conscience directs, and (3) seek to promote justice in specific situations.

More and more we hear from Christian pulpits a plea for confronting the problem "to determine the mind of Christ" and "to seek to do the will of God." My simple three-point exhortation was quoted widely by Southern newspapers, including Baptist publications. Many Baptists in the deep South would prefer not to have the topic discussed, but they are gradually (at least in some areas) being sensitized to the problem. Even though politically they vote "segregationist," they are generally willing for the denominational leadership to struggle with the problem. The Southern Baptist Convention, though historically all white, now includes some participating bi-racial churches and all-Negro churches.

Because of our congregational government, I have felt we should be extremely cautious in issuing statements that might indicate that Baptists uniformly support the Supreme Court decision. Our principal service is to encourage our constituents to make systematic studies of Bible teachings on the subject of race, primarily to provide instruction on what the Bible does *not* teach. One purpose, of course, is to counter the contention that segregation has biblical sanction. But never has Baptist literature carried even an insinuation that one is not Christian who opposes the Supreme Court decision or the official statements of the Southern Convention.

Ministers are sometimes reproached with this comment: "Don't let the preachers say that the schools should integrate till they integrate their own churches." This disregards (1) the fact that one seldom encounters a minister advocating desegregation who does not also advocate abandonment of race as a criterion for church membership, and (2) the more vital point that churches are not supported by tax revenues and are wholly private institutions with a clear right to base admission upon any standard the group determines. To recognize the right of a congregation to restrict its membership is quite consistent with the argument that the use of public facilities should be governed by the Bill of Rights. The right not to be turned away from a tax-supported public facility solely on grounds of race or color is quite a different thing from the privilege of joining a church or a private organization.

A survey of Negro opinion develops striking unanimity in these matters. Negroes, even those who prefer all-Negro schools, do not want color to be an official barrier in school enrollment, but most of them are disinterested in challenging valid tests for admission. It is legal segregation, not voluntary separateness, to which they object. A Texas Baptist preacher told me that a fellow minister, a Negro, once asked him, "Whatever gave you folks the crazy idea that we want to come over to your churches. We've got just as good a building as you have and we owe nothing on it, which is a whole lot less than you do."

In the South it is true that the church is literally everywhere. In communities that have witnessed the vanishing of their schools through the merger of districts, post offices, and stores, the little church remains—feeble and poorly supported, but a symbol of the people's aspiration for a better life here and hereafter. From churches, even in these remote

places and certainly in the populous centers, has stemmed an
influence for better race relations. It is evident that the
awakened conscience of Southern churches will make this
influence even more effective in the future. The ringing
statement on non-discrimination approved by the Southern
Presbyterians at the 1957 Birmingham meeting is in sharp
contrast with the Southern Presbyterian Assembly's 1864
statement: "We hesitate not to confirm that it is the peculiar
mission of the Southern church to conserve the institution of
slavery."

I have emphasized the role of the Southern Baptists in the
field of race relations because of my personal identification
with that faith, not because I intended to slight the work of
any other faith. Many faiths showed that willingness to com-
municate urged by Paul in I Timothy 6:18 when the Richmond Ministers Association issued, early in 1957, an outstanding statement of the moral responsibilities of Virgini-
ans, dealing with all aspects of the segregation problem. One
point that especially appealed to me was this: "We believe
that until a final satisfactory solution is achieved, every effort
should be made to make available to both white and colored
people the finest in educational and cultural advantages;
that wherever possible, and as rapidly as possible, social
custom violating the dignity of the Negro should be eradi-
cated. The passing away of these irritating customs does not
involve intermarriage or amalgamation of the races; it de-
clares a wholesome respect for all people and evidences common courtesy."

Billy Graham asks us to remember this simple eloquent
example:

"Shortly after the close of the Civil War, a Negro entered
a fashionable church in Richmond, Virginia, one Sunday
morning while communion was being served. He walked
down the aisle and knelt at the altar. A rustle of shock and

anger swept through the congregation. Sensing the situation, a distinguished layman immediately stood up, stepped forward to the altar and knelt beside his colored brother. Captured by his spirit, the congregation followed this magnanimous example.

"The layman who set the example was Robert E. Lee."

CHAPTER EIGHT

The Look Beyond

IN THEIR PRESENT DISTRESS OF MIND, MANY SOUTHERNERS ARE asking questions. What can be done to avoid violence? How can the schools that are subject to court orders to integrate be kept open in the face of state laws that require closing? Can any modification of the 1954 decision by the Supreme Court itself be anticipated? Is Congress likely to adopt effective measures of repeal?

A smaller number of Southerners are looking beyond these questions to other vital ones. How can communication between the races be re-established and be made useful in achieving peace and justice? How can the maximum contentment for the white majority be achieved in areas where changed patterns may be necessary for compliance? What is needed to assure the Negro minority of that dignity of position, without which it cannot make the contribution to the region of which it is capable? How can the lowering of standards of established schools for white children be avoided in the process of complying with the decision's minimum requirements?

We members of Congress from Southern states have the responsibility of interpreting developments in Washington to our people. Perhaps we have not worked hard enough at the job. While we have been struggling with many involved problems affecting the health and welfare of our constituents, some political leaders at home have been vigorously concentrating on race questions. I fear that this political activity has been a contributing influence to the temporary destruction of the racial good will and the democratic spirit which sustain free discussion of public questions. The result is a postponing of a solution to the nation's number one domestic problem. Frankness should require us to advise our constituents that there is scarcely any hope at all of a reversal of the 1954 decision of the Supreme Court. At least, the general principle upon which the decision rests will stand. While we can surmise that the justices themselves have been surprised at the extent of resistance and, if rendering a decision on the same basic questions today, might construe the Constitution in a more perceptive way, we know that there will be little concession from the nation's highest court to local resistance. My own hope is that the Court will, nevertheless, not deviate from the policy of granting wide discretion to the district judges.

I am also convinced that the Congress will not take any action in this field. While Congress has not hesitated to substitute its own judgment for that of the Court in the realm of policy, national legislators have distinguished between rulings that yield to statutes subsequently enacted (as in tidelands oil) and the defining of Constitutional rights (as in the desegregation decision) which can be changed only by Constitutional amendment. Respect for our oath of office, as well as an acknowledgment of the futility of such a course, would deter us. Moreover, there are strong political influences in the national picture that account for the obvious reluctance of the Congress to deal with this problem. The large and highly organized Negro vote in key states, such as New York, Pennsylvania, Ohio, Illinois, Michigan and

California (representing 181 electoral votes to 117 electoral votes of the eleven Southern states), is naturally sought by both national parties, and neither party organization—no matter how strong the pressures from the deep-South states—will take a stand in favor of setting aside the Court's rulings.

There is much to ponder in the fact that in at least eight Southern states opposition of the white majority to troop use was virtually unanimous, and vehemently so. Also much to be pondered is the near unanimity in the other forty states on the point that defiance should not be permitted. Not in modern times, perhaps, has the nation been so sharply divided along geographical lines as in this instance.

And political elements must be taken into account. We who oppose military enforcement of school integration are finding that our cause is not served appreciably by pointing out that there is a large element of politics in the Washington decisions. If the political pressures coincide with what an executive concludes, correctly or incorrectly, his duty requires, he is not likely to act differently just to avoid being charged with playing politics. After all, we live under a political system.

The pressures upon all three departments of government, judicial, executive, and legislative, that spring from areas outside the South, while providing support for the current school rulings, are nevertheless not producing any additional complications for the South. I believe the overwhelming majority of Northern people, for example, are eager to avoid placing strains upon national unity. Our appeal to them must be to reason and reasonableness. If the nation is to impose judgments upon Southern communities, those judgments should be mature and should be measured by the standards of our dual form of government. If we ourselves exercise greatest wisdom, perhaps they will be so measured. Surely, the Little Rock story proves the wisdom of James Madison's observation that our duality can succeed only if there be "reciprocal forbearance."

We of the white South have probably never fully appreciated the fact that there are expanding sympathies among the people of other regions and that, along with their insistence upon court compliance, they are responding to our appeal for an understanding attitude. A New Englander once said to me, "If I write an autobiography, I shall call it *Up from Abolition*."

We white Southerners, who have ourselves cultivated an interest in peoples "up North" and elsewhere, can hardly afford to persist in inconsistencies that would repel the involvement of others in our own conflicts. This is particularly true when we pause to consider how often the interest of others is expressed by gifts to our institutions and an apparent effort to understand the complexities of our problem. Above all, it is time for patience on the part of all concerned, because each side of the usual cleavages, white and Negro, North and South, liberal and conservative, has something to ask forgiveness for and should at the same time be forgiving. This is not to suggest that justice and truth are found in the golden mean and that the extremists are always wrong. Truth is sometimes an extreme partisan. Justice often lays a heavy burden upon its reluctant devotees. Insight, intelligence, and devotion are indispensable props for men of good will struggling with these problems of adjustment.

I recall what the old man from the hills said to the judge in Little Rock, who periodically had to sentence him to prison for violating the liquor laws: "Mr. Smith, you have again been found guilty of violating the law, and, before sentencing you the court wants to say that you and your boys have given this court more trouble than all the other people in Arkansas put together. Do you have anything to say?" "Yes, your Honor," the aged defendant said, "I just want to say that we haven't given you any more trouble than you've given us."

The thing that all regions must strive for is a national structure which permits of major differences and yet provides a basic foundation of principles and programs on which all can agree. Both our federal government and our major political parties reflect these apparently contradictory elements, in a synthesis that guarantees the rights of all minorities. Dr. Ernest S. Griffith comments that we have, as it were, a "government by consensus." By this he means that "no one group can have its way unless it can carry with it substantial fractions from each of the other great groups." With regard to the race question, Dr. Griffith considers it possible that "even the minority-rights program of the Negro may seek and find a middle ground as at least a temporary stage—such as the program of Representative Hays of Arkansas—which will command a measure of support even in the South, and the tradition and practice of government by consensus will again be demonstrated and vindicated." It was this desire that motivated me to present the Arkansas Plan for Civil Rights as a rallying ground for men of good will of all races in every section of the country, and it is this desire that continues to motivate me to help my beloved Southland find a way out of its current dilemma.

I doubt very much, however, that we can find the kind of consensus Dr. Griffith speaks of, if, in the field of race relations, we continue to permit our emotions to rule us. We have been facing two silences in the South, the silence of the aspiring Negro and the silence of the anxious white, and we must permit both to be heard in freedom and in safety. While the roar beyond their silences is indeed a deafening one, it tends to be smothered by a blanket of suspicion on all sides.

Moral elements in the present conflict are inescapable. They lie outside legal formulation but are influential. In assessing the sources of my own moral convictions, I often think back on my early upbringing. My mother had continually emphasized the importance of treating all human beings with dignity and compassion. In these closing pages of my story, I think I should share with you my impressions of an intimate family experience which forced me to confront the question of avoiding a hurt to Negro people that results from forced segregation in a meeting place. My mother's funeral (1955) was conducted in the church of my boyhood where my first instructions in Christian brotherhood were received. When one of the Negro friends of my mother asked me where she should sit when she attended the funeral, it caused me to weigh this delicate question. I tried to take every factor into account, even the feelings of some who would regard my plan of seating as quixotic and improper. I am sure I was right in my conclusion, however. I conveyed my feelings to the pastor of the church about as follows:

"My mother had Negro friends and some of them want to attend her funeral. They have not suggested a nonsegregated service, but I know their feelings, and I know what my mother's feelings were about such matters. This is partly your responsibility since the congregation has made you its leader—it is your building—but it is partly my responsibility, too, because, while the public is invited, it is a family service. Regardless of community custom, would you mind telling the ushers to let the Negroes sit anywhere they wish?" The minister nodded, and I presume the undertaker who was listening to our talk complied, though he looked a bit skeptical. This was not a whim nor was it a mere demonstration of what I deemed were sociological values, it was purely an application of Christian principles as I interpret them.

The churches of the Southern Baptist Convention and other churches that I am familiar with have what is called the function of reconciliation. Southern Baptists have a broad fellowship and even include a few bi-racial congregations; thus to commit us to one course of action is not in accord with our tradition. We have a tremendous service to render in getting men to love and respect each other while they differ. Religious resources of all faiths and denominations can be used to establish better bridges of understanding between the races and appeal to the finest instincts of brotherhood of both white and Negro Southerners.

The South really has few prejudiced white people who cannot be persuaded to support justice and Christian charity. Above the shouting of hate-fomenting groups are the quiet voices of dedicated men and women who are eager for the Negro to enjoy progress and the full advantage of our Christian civilization. (The white tenant on my thirty-acre tract once said, "I believe in civilization. I always have. I like it that way.")

In the transition period we are undergoing before the achievement of a new equilibrium, the churches and religious leaders have already had an enormous role to play. In this regard, I should like to quote a statement issued by the Southern Baptist Christian Life Commission: "We urge Christian statesmen and leaders to use their leadership in positive thought and planning, to the end that this crisis in our national history shall not be made the occasion for new and bitter prejudices, but a movement toward a united nation embodying and proclaiming a democracy that will commend freedom to all peoples."

The Christian answer to the plea for simple justice in particular situations must not be diluted by the irrelevancy, "If granted this, he'll want something we could not and should not grant him."

In the struggle toward moral solutions, the moderate is to play an important part. Much has been written lately about the plight of the political moderate. True, he is caught between two highly vocal groups that entertain strong feelings. But there are many moderates among that multitude of segregationists in the deep South who, when free to speak without inhibition, will confess to having a sensitive conscience and a dissatisfaction with the total picture of today. "Some changes should be made," they agree.

Out of the past come voices of respected Southern statesmen. On the question of interposition (in the present context, clearly just another word for nullification), President Andrew Jackson said, in substance, to the people of his native state of South Carolina: "There are two things to be shown before invoking the revolutionary doctrine of nullification. First, are you right about your protest; are you in a strong moral position, resting your case upon a clear proof of injustice and usurpation? And second, have you the force to resist the force that must be set against a state's defiance of the nation's authority?"

Passing over the matter of the moral strength of the resistance movement, it is clear that no single state has the resources to resist federal decrees that really represent the judgment and feelings of a significant majority of the people of the country.

While, as I have said, truth is sometimes partisan and even relentlessly immoderate, still the moderates are indispensable in the long and continuous struggle for race harmony. Analogies to the Civil War are not always accurate. However, we can see a little better, after the clash of opinion and feeling today, how Lincoln and Lee were driven away from middle ground. The extremists on both sides denied the people the only alternatives to violence.

While the elements of hatred and prejudice cannot be denied to exist in limited areas of our society, any indictments based upon those motivations should be narrowly drawn. Not many people really hate, but many people are in mortal fear of changes in race patterns, and fear is akin to hate. But hatred is not the principal difficulty. The political representative has a real problem here. He is duty bound to take the fears of people into account. I do not mean that he should expect to allay them completely but that the existence of fears, though unfounded, creates a condition that must be reckoned with.

The fears of change by the white majority and the aspirations for change by the Negro minority apply pressures on the political system. Sometimes they impinge upon the conscience and mind of a single representative.

The antidote for fear is fact, and the educational and religious leadership of the nation must busy itself in the dissemination of facts on this subject. If, for example, the utterly false interpretation of the Bible teachings, currently finding an audience in some sections of the South, could be corrected, we would be able to take a long forward step toward a solution to the school integration problem.

The ethical and moral aspects of the conflict are in the long run more important than the legal and political phases. Even the word integration, which has become (to use Justice Brandeis' phrase) a conjure word, does not express either the Negro's basic hope or the Court's intention. It is to achieve non-discrimination that the minority is really seeking. That is the basis for the Supreme Court's decisions in 1954 and 1955, as I interpret them.

A fact often overlooked is that the Court did not order integration. The decision did not require the admission of a student to a school of his choosing or force any child to attend a particular school. What it did hold is that no child may be excluded from a school solely because of race. The Negroes in the South would perhaps be willing to abandon some demands and, without much protest, accept in return the slight alterations in segregation patterns that would result from localities adopting the following criteria (I believe they are sufficient to eliminate discrimination):

1. Residential. Negro students should not be required to travel to schools beyond the limits of their own residential areas if schools are maintained for others in the same areas.

2. Specialized Courses. If a Negro student qualifies for special courses not available in the Negro school, he should be admitted to the course along with the white students pursuing such specialization. This formula accounts for the assignment of some of the nine students to Central High in Little Rock.

3. High Scholastic Standing. Here it seems that the lag in educational advancement of the Negro should be recognized. One argument against rapid integration is that both white and Negro students are handicapped when they are thrown together on a large scale. However, exceptional Negro students are discriminated against if they are not admitted to the white school of the same neighborhood which, for whatever cause, is able to maintain higher standards.

My concern over the failure of the federal government to stress reliance on the local area to provide such solutions extends to the state level and to the regional level. This means: (1) no community in a state should tell another how to cope with its racial problems; (2) a state government should occupy a fair and impartial role (not cutting off funds in school districts that elect to integrate, as is threatened in Virginia, South Carolina, and elsewhere); and, (3) above all, no state in the South should tell another what to do in its attempts to preserve law and order.

It can, of course, be seen that everything is not quite as satisfactory as it might be at the local level. In the old order, it has required imagination and study for the Negroes to achieve advantages in relation to their white friends. Since so much depends upon decisions of white men in a society dominated by them, the Negro, in seeking happiness and security, has to some extent "lived by his wits." It is an old saying that "a Negro who doesn't have a white man for a friend is a fool, and a white man who doesn't have a Negro for a friend is a mighty poor manager." The consequences of this relation have been apparent. They belonged to a phase of the Negro's progress as a maturing segment of American society. This has carried some advantages to the race—in short, he adjusted. There were, however, and in places there are still, some discouragements to growth and responsibility. Perhaps you heard of the Negro elevator operator's response when a passenger asked, "Why are you always so cheerful and so patient? You don't get excited; you never show irritation." He answered, "Well, it's this way. I never let the little things bother me, and I don't mess with the big things at all." He is being told today, however, by the prominent leaders of his race that he must concern himself with some of the big things. The easy way of leaving all of the decisions to the white people has to be abandoned. Events are forcing a change. Again, this is a phase of our maturing in democratic government. One can find daily evidences of the fact that Negroes have an avid and continuing interest in political and legislative activities. Negro representation in the Congress during my tenure has risen from one to four.

This leads me to the question: "What does the Negro really want in the present situation?" No one but the Negro himself can answer that question, and he is entitled to be heard. I anticipate that we shall find him asking first of all that no law, even by implication, give him an inferior status and that he not be legally segregated in any of the public services. At the center of the whole controversy is his determination to defend his dignity peacefully. It is *official* segregation, not separatism, to which he objects. I have never heard a single criticism by a Negro (though I have heard it from white people) of the general practice of Southern white churches in restricting their membership. The right of private organizations to determine membership is a part of the free way of life, and the Negro recognizes that.

The Negro has had to pay a big price for the gains he achieved under the Supreme Court school decisions. White Southerners have reacted violently, not only in Little Rock, but elsewhere in the South, and the race harmony, which until the 1954 and 1955 decisions had enabled the builders of good will in both races to work without hindrance, has been somewhat undermined by the wave of emotion created by forced integration. There is some evidence that NAACP officials are aware of this. Voluntary suspension of litigation may accomplish more than efforts toward official Congressional or Supreme Court action to win a respite for areas where feelings of resistance are high. It is unfortunate, however, that the decision of this private organization (not accountable to any public authority) not to litigate in certain states is all that stands between some communities and potential violence.

I do not believe I have exaggerated the importance of the clergyman in the processes of wholesome change. As he listens sympathetically to the minority's plea, he must have a keen sensitivity to the needs of his own congregation. He should not think of social action exclusively in vocal terms, nor should he press such action on a community that requires time and a spontaneous willingness. It is in this spirit that he can be tolerant of those White Citizens Councils that strive to maintain the old order without violence but with the mighty influence of public opinion. While some of the members are rabble-rousers and publicity seekers, many others are sincere, well-educated citizens who represent the best elements in the community and repeatedly renounce violence. They might well have joined these groups simply because of the sincere belief that the Supreme Court exceeded its authority in declaring invalid the state statutes requiring racial segregation. There are some who have joined because they are convinced that desegregation would destroy social principles and values in which they believe. In any event, they represent a significant sector of the Southern population which can be reasoned with and which should not be discounted in the process of resolving current difficulties.

The issues that remain to be resolved in the area of race relations are many, but I trust the story I have told will give the thoughtful citizen reason to hope for real progress towards a new equilibrium. The school segregation decisions have caused the development of two streams of traffic moving in opposite directions. We who are on the white line down the middle have often felt lonesome and frightened, but, as more and more people have joined us, we are beginning to feel that it will not be long before almost everyone is moving in the same direction again. The decisions cannot now be recalled, but they can be interpreted in a way that will preserve the rule-of-law tradition and still meet with acceptance in the South.

A long second look at the 1954 and 1955 Supreme Court decisions should convince local leaders in scattered communities which are pressured to comply that great flexibility is in the decisions. This fact, coupled with the known desire of Negro leaders in those localities to live in harmony and mutual respect with their white neighbors, will produce a satisfactory situation. (The various methods of compliance that might be adopted without loss of values deemed vital by the white majority, such as establishment of schools segregated by sex, have frequently been mentioned.)

The white leadership of the South must strengthen the hands of influential leaders within the Negro community who, while fully alert to the Negroes' aspirations, are free from subservience to national pressure groups. Such leaders are available if white leaders would begin to enlist them in building bridges between the two communities.

Largely untapped is the reservoir of good will in the colleges. For example, one of the most articulate and active spokesmen for reason and moderation in the South is Colgate W. Darden, Jr., President of the University of Virginia. He is not advocating full integration but rather the continuation of the dual system throughout the state, with most Negroes voluntarily attending predominantly Negro schools, even though the doors of white schools may be open to them. There can be no doubt that a leading voice of sanity in the search for a peaceful solution of Virginia's problem has been that of Mr. Darden.

Trustworthy and proven Negro leaders are the ones needed to carry the minority's responsibility, not the "white man's Negro," who long ago lost his following among the minority. Firm contacts with this Negro leadership must inevitably restore harmony in the region, because we would then have at the grass roots level in the community the authentic statements of purpose and aspiration which can be communicated by Negroes to their white neighbors. This process would do much to break down the suspicions which are fostered by ignorance and misunderstanding.

One of my purposes in writing this book has been to plead for acceptance of these three principles: (1) the Constitutional rights of all children (as distinguished from the social aspirations of their elders) must be recognized and enforced, though this will mean some altered patterns (the *American* idea); (2) the determination of educational policies to achieve a non-violent application of those Constitutional rights must rest finally to a large degree on the individual communities, and the states must not thwart that determination (the *Jeffersonian* idea); and (3) the influences that work both inside and outside the political and governmental systems for equality and justice must have both a tireless devotion to these ideals and an attitude of love and patience (the *Christian* idea).

The policy of the federal government should be devised to deal imaginatively with the new situation. This means a heavy reliance on the local sense of justice and fair play to create an environment where brotherhood and harmony between the races can flourish. Attempts to force legal doctrines on the region that cannot be reconciled with the beliefs of the people are doomed to failure. What can be done is to give the minority group a "psychological release" from the oppressive continuance of legal discrimination by gradual removal of formal barriers. The pattern of race relations that the federal government could then encourage would be created on a voluntary basis and would permit the *natural* separation that would occur without psychological damage to the Negro.

I close now with a plea to the South and to the nation for faith in the success of our mission to defend democracy in our land and throughout the free world. The question of civil rights is only a small segment of the total complex of values of our Christian civilization.

It is the threatened loss of faith in something, the unsureness about what we believe, that requires a contribution from the Christian community. I doubt that we can survive without strengthening this element in the life of the South. We must, therefore, create an atmosphere of friendliness to the ideal itself, which is a sense of destiny and a belief in the divine purposes in human existence. When we are through defining the beliefs that we hold in common—beliefs about man, about God, the creator and the righteous judge, and about justice in human relations and the quest for freedom for all men—there will still be plenty of issues to be submitted to the people for decision. The re-evaluation of our faith, the re-defining of goals, and the new resolutions, which we as a free people must form to acquire the strength for resisting those who put their confidence in materialism and power, are things which must occupy us in the next few years, else we will lose the world conflict and all the human rights we so deeply cherish.